Excel
MADE EASY

A beginner's guide including how-to skills and projects

Ewan Arthur

ARCTURUS

This edition published in 2013 by Arcturus Publishing Limited
26/27 Bickels Yard, 151–153 Bermondsey Street,
London SE1 3HA

The materials in this book relate to Microsoft Office 2010.

Prepared for Arcturus by Starfish Design Editorial and Project
Management Ltd.

ISBN: 978-1-84858-419-8
AD001922US

Printed in China

Contents

How to use this book

This book will help you learn how to use Microsoft **Excel**, probably the most popular spreadsheet software in the world.

- It is written for beginners and covers only what you really need.

- There's no jargon, just simple instructions and lots of pictures. You'll start with the basics and soon be able to make tables and charts, do math and manage money.

- Every left-hand page is called *How to do it* and teaches a new <u>skill</u>. Every right-hand page is called *Using it* and has a fun exercise to <u>practice</u> that skill.

HOW TO DO IT

This page explains each skill and the steps needed to use it.
Pictures show you what's on your computer screen.

USING IT

These exercises make up a series of projects. The *Using it* pages also have simple step-by-step stages with pictures.

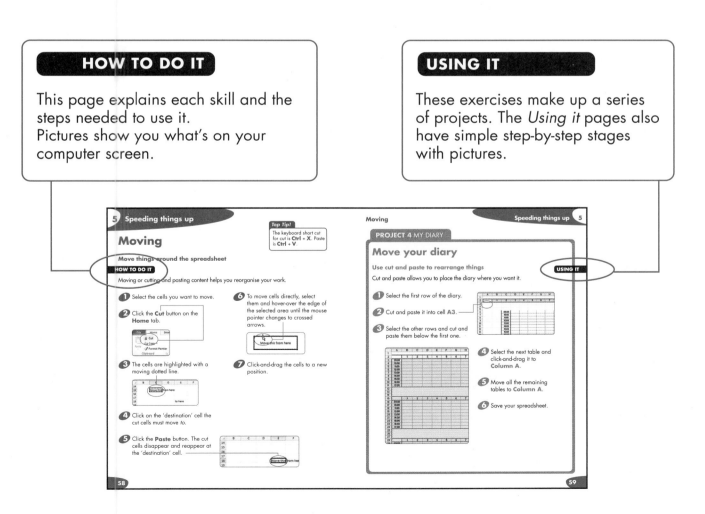

The Microsoft Office Excel window

What you will see when you open **Excel**:

The **Office** button. Click this to do things to the whole document such as save it. You can also customize how **Excel** works.

The **Quick Access toolbar** – does most common tasks such as Open and Save, but without any options.

The **Ribbon** – is where most of the options that you will learn about are found.

The **Formula Bar** – shows you the calculation (formula), number or text inside a cell.

The **Close** button. Click to exit **Excel**.

The **Name Box** – shows a cell's address. Type a cell name here too.

A **Spreadsheet** – where you do your work. Also called a **Workbook**.

The **Scroll Bars** – let you move across and down the spreadsheet.

Worksheet Tabs. You can have several worksheets in a spreadsheet. View them by clicking the tabs.

Row and **Column Headers** – show the row number and column letter of a cell's address.

The **Zoom Slider** – lets you see parts of your document up close.

Cells. The spreadsheet is organized as a grid of boxes called cells.

The ribbon

The **ribbon** is where to find most of the tools you use. It is divided into several **tabs**. Each tab is split up into sets of tools. **Excel** is clever and, depending on what you are working on, useful tabs will appear in the ribbon. This means what you see will often change.

Highlighting – this shows which buttons are currently in use.

A **Button drop-down menu** – shows options related to a button.

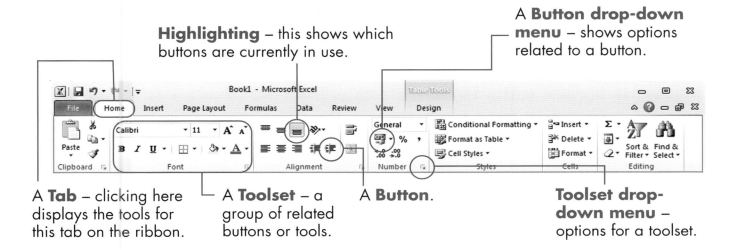

A **Tab** – clicking here displays the tools for this tab on the ribbon.

A **Toolset** – a group of related buttons or tools.

A **Button**.

Toolset drop-down menu – options for a toolset.

Starting Excel

What to do to get **Excel** running on your computer.

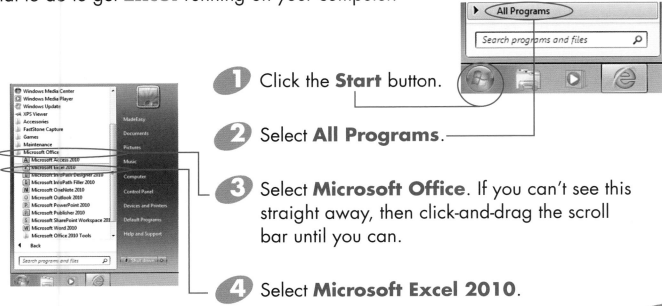

1 Click the **Start** button.

2 Select **All Programs**.

3 Select **Microsoft Office**. If you can't see this straight away, then click-and-drag the scroll bar until you can.

4 Select **Microsoft Excel 2010**.

Using the mouse

You will use a mouse and keyboard with **Excel**. You can often use either to do the same thing. For example, you can get help by pressing the **F1** function key or clicking the (?) icon.

Common terms and techniques

Right-click – press and release the <u>right</u>-hand button.

Click – press and release the <u>left</u>-hand button. Two quick clicks is a **Double-Click**.

Click-and-drag – press the left mouse button, move (or drag) the cursor and then release it. This either highlights everything covered or moves whatever was selected by the first click.

Mouse pointer – moving the mouse moves the mouse pointer around the screen. It changes depending on what is going on.

Cursor – the flashing line (cursor) shows where type will appear when entered.

Hover-over – keep the mouse pointer over a button for a few seconds. This will often produce a pop-up help message.

Using the keyboard

Common terms and techniques

Esc – closes any pop-up windows and menus you don't want any more.

Caps Lock – when pressed, everything is typed in capital letters.

Function Keys – can be used as shortcuts for tools and options. The **F7** key brings up the spelling checker.

Backspace – deletes text to the <u>left</u> of the cursor.

Delete – deletes text to the <u>right</u> of the cursor.

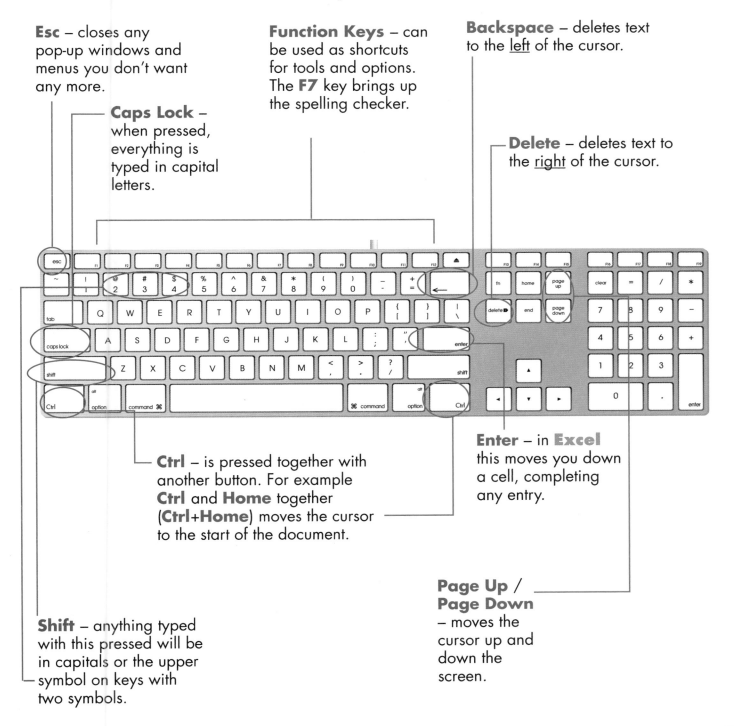

Ctrl – is pressed together with another button. For example **Ctrl** and **Home** together (**Ctrl+Home**) moves the cursor to the start of the document.

Enter – in **Excel** this moves you down a cell, completing any entry.

Shift – anything typed with this pressed will be in capitals or the upper symbol on keys with two symbols.

Page Up / Page Down – moves the cursor up and down the screen.

Launching Excel

Creating and **Saving** workbooks

HOW TO DO IT

Top Tip!

Use New folder in the "Save As" dialog box to organize your spreadsheets.

1 Click on the **File** tab.

2 Click on **New** to view the new Workbook options.

3 Double-click on "Blank Workbook."

4 Click on a cell in the new speadsheet, type something and press the **Enter** key.

5 To save the workbook, click **Save** in the **File** tab.

🖫 Save

6 A dialog box opens. A default name "Book 1" is given to your file, but you should give it a name that helps identify it. Then click **Save**.

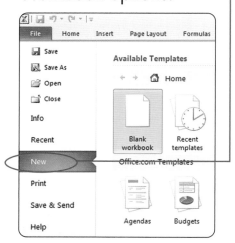

PROJECT 1 TO-DO LIST

A simple first spreadsheet

Create a workbook, add your to-dos and save it

USING IT

Start a spreadsheet, add information and save it.

1 Open a new spreadsheet.

2 Enter your first to-do in cell **B4**.

3 Press the **Enter** key. This will move you to the cell below, **B5**.

4 Add your other jobs to your list.

	A	B	C	D
1				
2				
3				
4	Monday	Clean shoes		
5	Saturday	Tidy room		
6	Friday	Guitar practice		
7	Today	Walk the dog		
8	Sunday	Write thank you letters		
9				
10				

5 Click on cell **A4** and enter the date when you have to do the to-do.

6 Save your work as *My Todo list 1*.

7 Close the spreadsheet and **Excel** using the **Close** button.

Opening existing workbooks

Open a workbook and **Save As** a different workbook

HOW TO DO IT

Your existing files may need to be copied.

Top Tip!

The **File** tab opens showing recent documents. Recent Double-click on these to open them.

1 Click on the **File** tab and then on the **Open** button.

2 A dialog box opens showing the **Excel** files in your *Documents* folder. Click on the workbook you want to use, then on the **Open** button.

3 Click on the **File** tab and then **Save As**.

4 In the "Save As" dialog box, click the **New folder** button to create a folder to save your files in. Name it *My spreadsheets*.

5 Change the "File name" to *Book 2*.

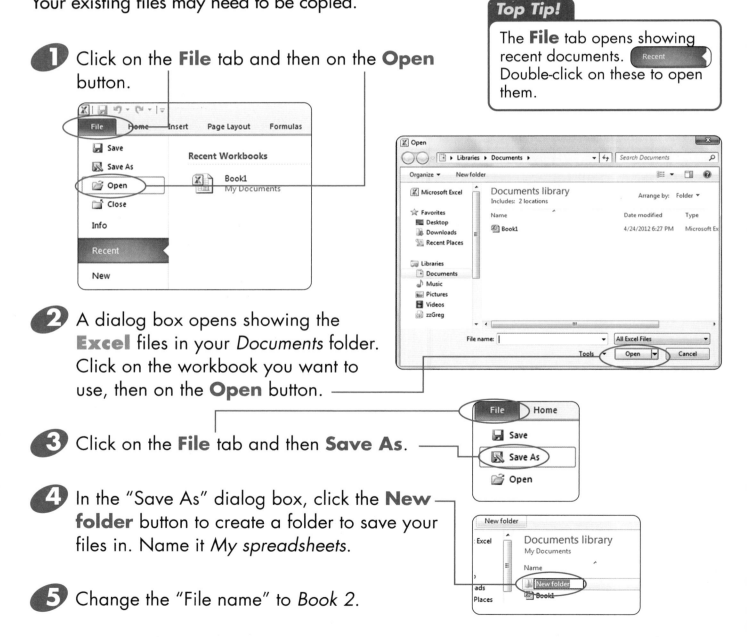

PROJECT 1 TO-DO LIST

Save a copy of your workbook

Take a copy so you can compare your changes

USING IT

Open a spreadsheet, add information and save it with a new name

1 Click on the **File** tab and **Open** button to open *My Todo list 1*.

2 From the **File** tab, click on **Save As**.

3 Create a new folder, "My to-do lists."

4 Change the file name to *My Todo list 2*.

5 Add more to-dos.

6 **Save** and **Close** the workbook.

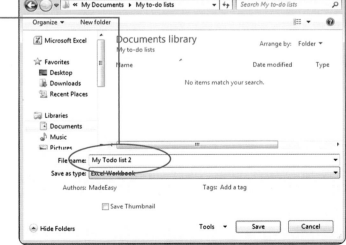

Using the cloud

Top Tip!

If you do not have a Windows Live ID, click on "Sign up for Windows Live" and follow the instructions.

Save your spreadsheet to the internet and open it again

HOW TO DO IT

If you save your work to the cloud you can open it from any computer with access to the internet and share it with other people.

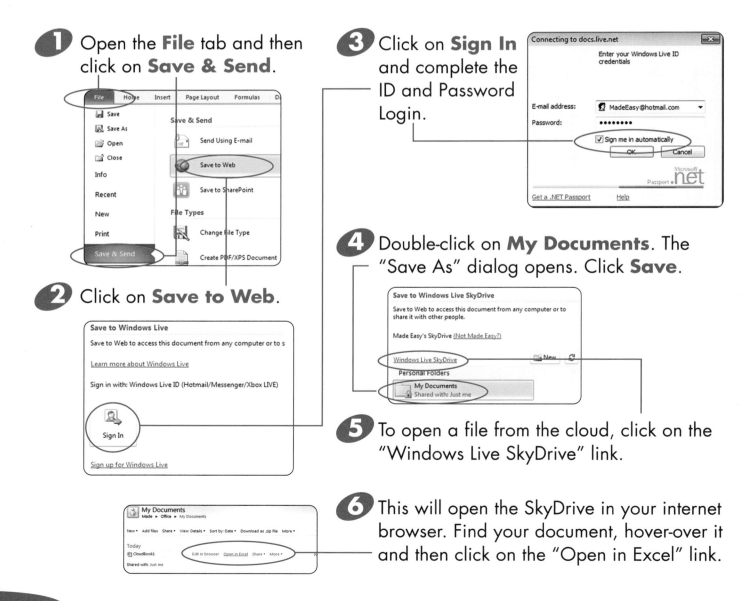

1 Open the **File** tab and then click on **Save & Send**.

2 Click on **Save to Web**.

Save to Windows Live

Save to Web to access this document from any computer or to s

Learn more about Windows Live

Sign in with: Windows Live ID (Hotmail/Messenger/Xbox LIVE)

Sign In

Sign up for Windows Live

3 Click on **Sign In** and complete the ID and Password Login.

Connecting to docs.live.net

Enter your Windows Live ID credentials

E-mail address: MadeEasy@hotmail.com

Password: ••••••••

☑ Sign me in automatically

OK   Cancel

Get a .NET Passport   Help

4 Double-click on **My Documents**. The "Save As" dialog opens. Click **Save**.

Save to Windows Live SkyDrive

Save to Web to access this document from any computer or to share it with other people.

Made Easy's SkyDrive (Not Made Easy?)

Windows Live SkyDrive   New

Personal Folders

My Documents
Shared with: Just me

5 To open a file from the cloud, click on the "Windows Live SkyDrive" link.

6 This will open the SkyDrive in your internet browser. Find your document, hover-over it and then click on the "Open in Excel" link.

My Documents
Made ▸ Office ▸ My Documents

New ▾ Add files Share ▾ View: Details ▾ Sort by: Date ▾ Download as .zip file More ▾

Today
CloudBook1   Edit in browser Open in Excel Share ▾ More ▾

Shared with: Just me

PROJECT 1 TO-DO LIST

Save your to-dos to the cloud

You can keep track of your to-dos anywhere

Use the cloud to store your todos and open them again.

1 Open your *My Todo list 1* spreadsheet.

2 **Sign in** to Windows Live.

3 Save your workbook to your *My Documents* folder in the SkyDrive.

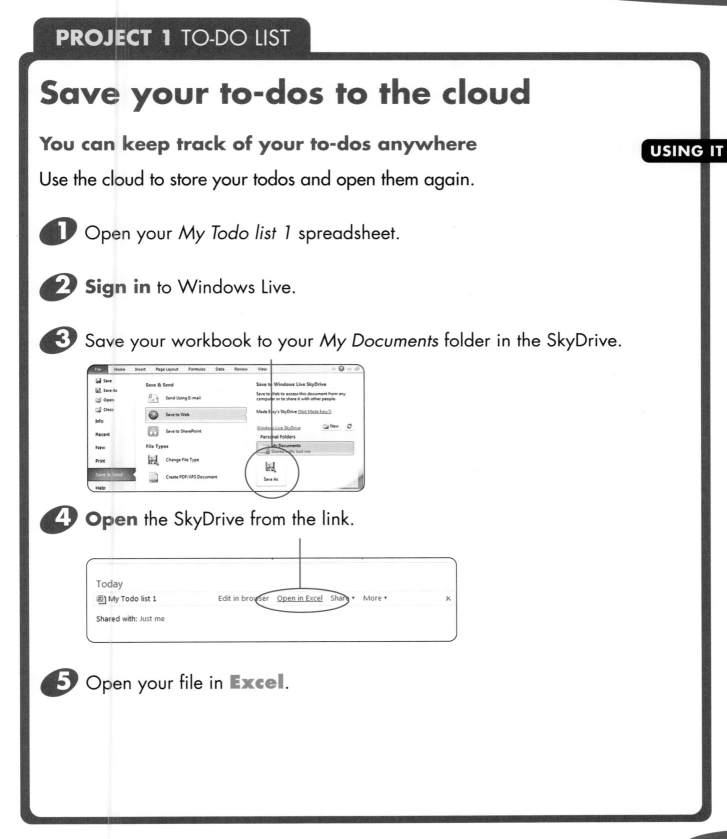

4 **Open** the SkyDrive from the link.

5 Open your file in **Excel**.

Moving around spreadsheets

Moving around and deleting using the mouse and keyboard

HOW TO DO IT

You will make mistakes. Here's how to move around a spreadsheet to delete things.

 Move from one cell to another by clicking in that cell or using the keyboard arrow keys.

Start Cell — Right arrow key 3 times

Down arrow 3 times

 Click-and-drag the "Scroll Bar" or press the **Page Up** or **Page Down** keys to move up and down.

 Press the **Delete** key to delete everything in a cell.

 Delete several cells by click-and-dragging the mouse pointer across them, then pressing the **Delete** key.

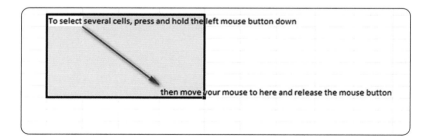

To select several cells, press and hold the left mouse button down

then move your mouse to here and release the mouse button

Top Tip!

Press the **Tab** key to move a cell to the right.

PROJECT 1 TO-DO LIST

Add and delete to-dos

Update your to-dos

USING IT

Delete the to-dos you have done and add new ones.

1 Open *My Todo list 2* from your Documents Library.

2 Move to the bottom and add new to-dos.

Monday	Clean shoes
Saturday	Tidy room
Friday	Guitar practice
Today	Walk the dog
Sunday	Write thank you letter

Top Tip!

The "Column Headers" and "Row Headers" highlight which cell you are in.

3 Delete any jobs you have completed.

Monday	Clean shoes
Saturday	Tidy room
Friday	Guitar practice
Today	Walk the dog
Sunday	Write thank you letters
Tuesday	Cook dinner
Friday	Math homework

4 Select all the new jobs and delete them.

3		
4	Monday	Clean shoes
5	Saturday	Tidy room
6	Friday	Guitar practice
7	Today	Walk the dog
8	Sunday	Write thank you letter
9	Tuesday	Cook dinner
10	Friday	Math homework
11		

More sheets

Top Tip!

Keep your worksheet names short or you won't be able to see them all.

Adding extra **Worksheets**

HOW TO DO IT

A blank **Excel** workbook has three worksheets, but you can have many more and name them to help keep track.

1 Move between worksheets by clicking on the **Worksheet** tab at the bottom of the window.

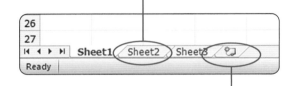

2 To add a new worksheet, click on the **Insert Worksheet** tab.

3 Give your sheet a name by right-clicking its tab and select **Rename**. Start typing your new name and press the **Enter** key.

4 If you no longer require it, right-click the tab and select **Delete**.

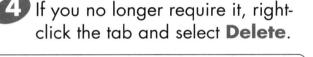

5 To reorganize your worksheets, click-and-drag the tab to the desired position. The **black arrow** shows where the sheet will be moved to.

PROJECT 1 TO-DO LIST

Add more worksheets to your to-do list

More worksheets mean you can list your to-dos for several weeks

Add worksheets and name them for a new to-do list for each week.

 Open your workbook *My Todo list 2* and rename the first worksheet *Week 1*.

> Week 1 │ Sheet2 │ Sheet3

2 Rename the other worksheets *Week 2* and *Week 3*.

> Week 2 │ Week 3 │ **Week 4** │ Sheet5

Challenge!

Right-click a worksheet tab and select the **Tab Color** option.

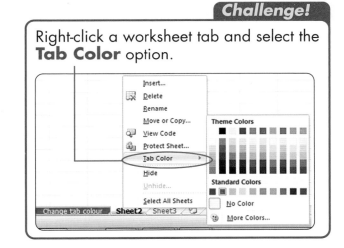

3 Add new worksheets *Week 4* and *Week 5*.

4 Add another worksheet. Call it *Repeat to-dos*. Move it to before *Week 1*.

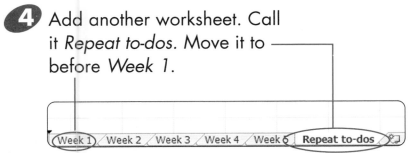

> Week 1 │ Week 2 │ Week 3 │ Week 4 │ Week 5 │ **Repeat to-dos**

First words

Cells and the Formula Bar

HOW TO DO IT

You can edit text once it is entered in a cell.

 Open a new spreadsheet.

 Click on a cell and type a sentence.

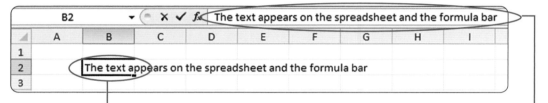

 The text appears both in the cell and the "Formula Bar."

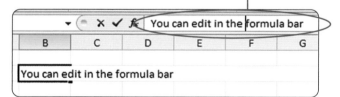 To edit a cell, double-click on the cell, press the **F2** key or click on the "Formula Bar."

Once editing a cell, use the **Arrow**, **Backspace** and **Delete** keys to move around.

Press the **Enter** key to finish.

Remember!

Click on cells or use the **Arrow** keys to move around spreadsheets.

PROJECT 2 REHEARSAL SCHEDULE

Create and edit your rehearsal schedule

Start a spreadsheet, add information and save it

1 Start a new workbook. Starting in cell **C6**, list the roles in your show.

	B	C	D	E
1				
2				
3				
4				
5				
6		Dorothy		Jane
7		Scarecrow		Peter
8		Tinman		Jose
9		Cowardly Lion		Aaron
10		Aunt Em		Melissa
11		Wicked Witch West	Zoya	
12		Wicked Witch East	Rebecca	
13		Uncle Henry		Carl
14		Wizard of Oz		Joseph
15				

2 Starting in **E6**, add the first names of who is going to play each role.

3 Edit each name to add their last name. Try using **F2**, clicking in the formula bar and double-clicking the cell.

| ✓ | fx | Jane Par |

	C	D	E	F
	Dorothy		Jane Par	
	Scarecrow		Peter	
	Tinman		Jose	

	C	D	E	F
	Dorothy		Jane Par	
	Scarecrow		Peter G	
	Tinman		Jose	
	Cowardly Lion		Aaron	
	Aunt Em		Melissa	

4 Save your workbook as "Rehearsal Schedule 1."

Series fun

Use **Auto Fill** to complete a series

 HOW TO DO IT

 Excel can complete series such as numbers and dates automatically.

1 Open a workbook. Type *1, 2, 3* in three cells.

2 Select these cells.

3 Hover-over the small square at the bottom right of your selection until the mouse pointer turns into the "Auto Fill" cross.

4 Click-and-drag the "Auto Fill" cross downwards. **Excel** automatically fills in the next numbers in the series.

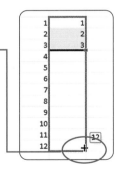

5 **Excel** can "Auto Fill" dates too. Type *Mon, Tue* then use "Auto Fill" to add the other five days of the week.

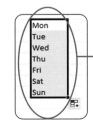

PROJECT 2 REHEARSAL SCHEDULE

Add the rehearsal dates

Quickly build up your schedule

Use "Auto Fill" to set your rehearsal dates and set the scenes.

 In cell **F5** add the date on which your rehearsals start.

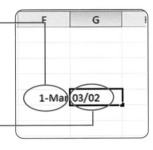

 Add the next date in cell **G5**.

3 Select **F5** and **G5**, then "Auto Fill" until you reach the dress rehearsal date.

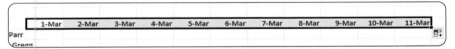

4 Type *1* in the cell above the dress rehearsal date, then *2* in the cell to the left.

5 Select the two cells and then "Auto Fill," but this time to the left, so we get a countdown of the number of days to go.

 Save your workbook.

Top Tip!

If you type in a date with just day and month, **Excel** will show the month, e.g. 1/01 will be shown as 01-Jan.

Fonts and points

Changing **Fonts** and **Font Sizes**

HOW TO DO IT

Fonts are styles of text. Each has a name and is measured in points. The standard size is 11 point, but you can go from 1 to 409 point.

1 Open a spreadsheet.

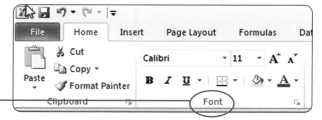

2 Go to the "Font" toolset on the **Home** tab. ——

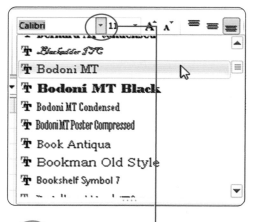

3 Click the **Font** button drop-down menu and select a new font.

Note **Excel** automatically makes rows bigger as you increase the font size.

4 Start typing in a cell. The text will appear in that font style.

5 To change the font of text already in a cell, select the cell then click the **Font** button drop-down menu and choose a new font.

6 To make a font bigger or smaller choose a new size using the **Font Size** button drop-down menu or click the **Grow Font** or **Shrink Font** buttons.

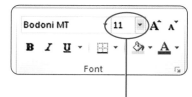

PROJECT 2 REHEARSAL SCHEDULE

Add a big title – size matters

Start to lay out your schedule

A big title and different fonts will help organize the schedule.

1 In cell **C2** type in the name of your show.

2 Select cell **C2** and change the font to *Playbill*.

3 Increase the font size to 36 point.

4 Select the dates and reduce the font to 9 point, using the **Shrink Font** button.

5 Change the font to *Arial Black*.

Styles

Style text with Bold, Italic, Underline, and Colors

HOW TO DO IT

"Bold," "italic," and "underline" make text stand out. Colors brighten things up.

1 Select a cell with text in. Click the **Bold** button on the **Home** tab. The text becomes **bold**.

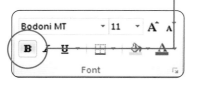

2 Click the **Italic** button to make text *italic*.

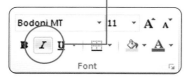

3 Click the **Underline** button to underline text.

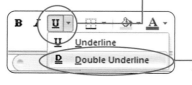

4 Choose different underline styles by selecting from the **Underline** button drop-down menu.

5 You can use all three styles (bold, italic, and underline) at the same time.

6 Text is normally black. The **Font Color** button drop-down menu lets you choose a different text color. Click the **Font Color** button to apply that color.

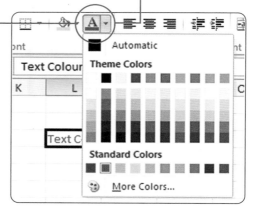

PROJECT 2 REHEARSAL SCHEDULE

A bit of style

Use font styles and colors

The rehearsal schedule lacks color.

1 Select the roles and click on the **Bold** button.

2 Select the title and make it **underlined**.

3 Make the title blue.

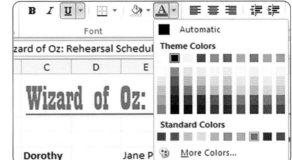

4 Make the countdown days italic.

5 Save your work.

Challenge!

Experiment with other text styles in the "Format Cells" dialog box. Click the "Font" toolset drop-down menu.

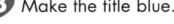

Left or right

Aligning, Merging, and Wrapping text in cells

HOW TO DO IT

Excel automatically starts <u>text</u> at the left of a cell and <u>numbers</u> and <u>dates</u> to the right. This is not always wanted.

1 Click the **Align Text Center** button in the **Home** tab to align text in the middle of a cell.

2 To move it to the right, click the **Align Text Right** button.

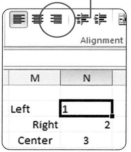

3 To type at different angles, use the **Orientation** button drop-down menu. This gives you several alignment choices.

4 Select **Format Cell Alignment** to set an exact angle, such as *30* degrees.

5 Sometimes you can't see all the text in a cell. Use the **Wrap Text** button to get several lines into one cell.

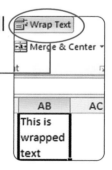

6 You can merge several cells into one. This can be useful for centering a heading above work. Select two or more cells and click the **Merge & Center** button. They become a single large cell.

PROJECT 2 REHEARSAL SCHEDULE

Align your schedule

Use alignment tools to layout the rehearsal schedule

Change the alignment of the different parts of the schedule.

1 Select the countdown days and left-align them.

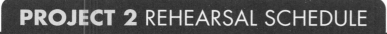

2 Select the dates and center them.

3 Select the cells in Row 3 from column C to above your last date. Click **Merge & Center** to center the title above your schedule.

Wizard of Oz: Rehearsal Schedule

11	10	9	8	7	6	5	4
1-Mar	2-Mar	3-Mar	4-Mar	5-Mar	6-Mar	7-Mar	8-M

Challenge!

Use the "Vertical Alignment" tools to position the roles to the top of their cells.

4 Select the names of the players and use **Wrap Text**.

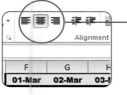

Set your table

Changing the **Row Height** and **Column Width**

Rows and column sizes can be changed to help work fit.

1 Place the mouse pointer between two row or column headers until it changes to a "Double Arrow" cursor.

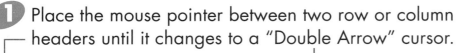

2 Click-and-drag the column or row to the size you want. A pop-up message will show how big it is.

3 You can change several columns or rows at once. Select all the columns or rows by click-and-dragging over the headers.

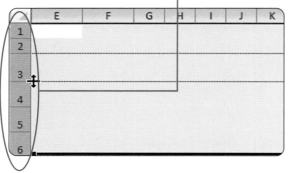

4 Then click-and-drag to resize <u>one</u> of the selected columns or rows. The others all change size too.

5 There are more options to size columns and rows in the "Cells" toolset on the **Home** tab.

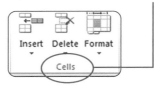

6 Select cells you want to change. Click the **Format** button drop-down menu and select **Row Height** or **Column Width**. A panel opens allowing you to set the height or width.

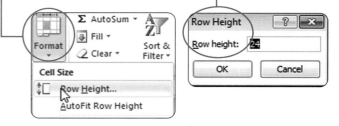

> **Top Tip!**
>
> Double-click on the edge of a column or row header to make it automatically fit to the largest cell in that column or row.

PROJECT 2 REHEARSAL SCHEDULE

Change column and row sizes to fit

There is a lot of wasted space – remove it

USING IT

Excel default sizes are not always what is needed for a clear layout.

1 Increase the width of the *Role* column to fit the largest role.

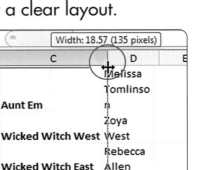

2 Increase the size of the *Player* column so that all names fit on two lines.

3 Use the **Cell Format** tool to make the *Names* rows the same height, 30 pixels.

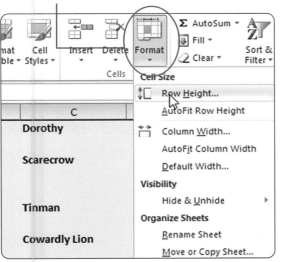

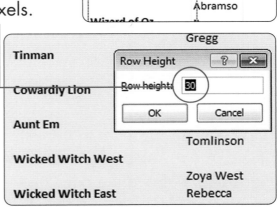

4 Make the date columns smaller: change the width to 60 pixels.

5 Save your workbook. Then save it as *Rehearsal Schedule 2*.

A bigger table

Inserting **Rows** and **Columns**

HOW TO DO IT

You will often have to add new columns and rows into a spreadsheet.

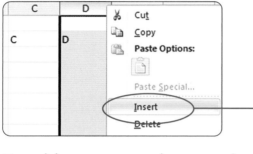

1 To add a row or column, right-click on a row or column header and select **Insert** from the pop-up menu.

C	Inserted Column	D	E

2 A new <u>column</u> appears to the <u>left</u> of the one you selected. A new <u>row</u> appears <u>above</u> the one you selected.

3 To add cells to a spreadsheet, click the **Insert** button in the "Cells" toolset of the **Home** tab.

4 Select the cell where you want a new cell added. Click the **Insert** button to insert a cell by moving all cells below it <u>down</u>.

5 Click the **Insert** button drop-down menu to see more options.

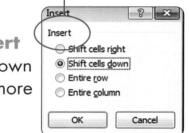

6 Select **Insert Cells** to see the "Insert" dialog box. Select the **Shift cells right** option and click OK to move cells to the <u>right</u> of the new cell.

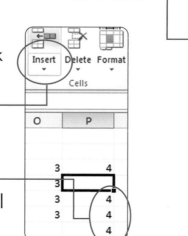

PROJECT 2 REHEARSAL SCHEDULE

Add rows and columns for more information

What else can we add to the rehearsal schedule?

Insert columns for the scenes and a row for what will be rehearsed.

 Open *Rehearsal Schedule 2*.

 Select the first five date columns and right-click a column header to view the pop-up menu.

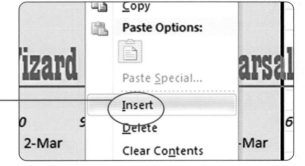

3 Select **Insert**, then add the scene names to each column.

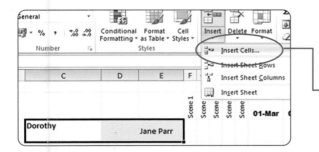

4 Align the scene text vertically and shrink the columns to fit.

5 Select the first role and name. Click on **Insert Cells** and select **Shift cells down**. Add titles to each column.

6 Save your work.

A smaller table

Deleting rows, columns and cells

HOW TO DO IT

Sometimes you need to remove cells from a spreadsheet.

 Right-click on the row or column header. Select **Delete**. ——————————

 The entire column is deleted.

 Delete cells by using the **Delete** button on the **Home** tab.

4 This moves cells below the deleted cell <u>up</u>.

5 To move cells from the right of the deleted cell to the <u>left</u>, click the **Delete** button drop-down menu, select **Delete Cells...** to bring up the "Delete" dialog box. Select the **Shift cells left** option, then click **OK**.

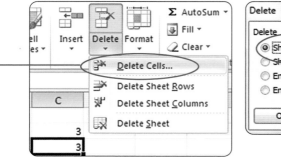

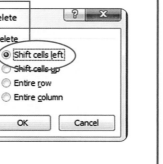

Top Tip!

Instead of deleting a row or column, you can hide it by right-clicking on the header and selecting **Hide** from the pop-up menu. To show the row or column again, select the headers either side and right-click, selecting **Unhide**.

Remove redundant rows and columns

USING IT

There is blank space in the schedule that you don't need

Deleting rows, columns, and cells will make the schedule more usable.

 Open *Rehearsal Schedule 2*.

 Right-click the **Column D** header. Select **Delete** from the pop-up menu.

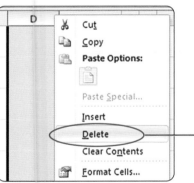

3 There are no rehearsals on 6 and 7 March. Select these dates and use the **Delete** tool to remove the cells.

 Select **Shift cells left** in the "Delete" dialog box to stop gaps in the schedule.

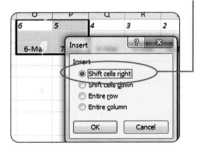

5 Save your work.

Sorting and reordering

Sorting lists into order

HOW TO DO IT

"Sorting" is one of the basic tools that make spreadsheets useful.
You can sort words, numbers and dates.

1 Type a list of fruits into a worksheet and select it.

	A
1	Pear
2	Banana
3	Mango
4	Apple
5	Lemon
6	Lime
7	Orange
8	Durian

2 Click the **Sort & Filter** button drop-down menu from the "Editing" toolset on the **Home** tab.

3 Select **Sort A to Z** to put the list into alphabetical order.

	A
1	Apple
2	Banana
3	Durian
4	Lemon
5	Lime
6	Mango
7	Orange
8	Pear

4 In the next column type the number of each fruit. Select the whole list.

5 Clicking the **Sort** button as above only sorts your list according to the <u>first</u> column. To sort by quantity (column **B**), select **Custom Sort** from the **Sort & Filter** button drop-down menu. The "Sort" dialog box appears.

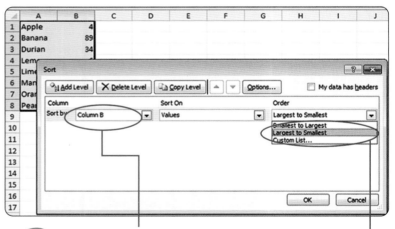

6 Select "Column B" from the **Sort by** drop-down menu then "Largest to Smallest" from the **Order** drop-down menu and click **OK**.
Your list is now ordered from largest to smallest number of fruit.

	A	B
1	Banana	89
2	Lime	76
3	Durian	34
4	Pear	22
5	Lemon	6
6	Apple	4
7	Mango	4
8	Orange	3

PROJECT 2 REHEARSAL SCHEDULE

Sort by cast member name

Use sorting to reorder the cast list and find who is required when

When you know who is required for each rehearsal, it is easier to get your actors to turn up!

1 Select the "Role" and "Player" columns, including the titles and use **Custom Sort** to sort by player name.

2 Make sure that the "My data has headers" option is ticked. Note that you can now sort by *Player* and not by *Column C*.

3 Mark which role is required for which scene using an "X."

4 Select *Role, Player* and *Scene* columns.

5 Use **Custom Sort** to show all the players required for Scene 3.

Make your table stand out

Add **Borders** to tables

HOW TO DO IT

You can make columns and rows stand out by using borders.

1 Open a new workbook. In the "Font" toolset on the **Home** tab, click the **Borders** button drop-down menu. Select **All Borders**.

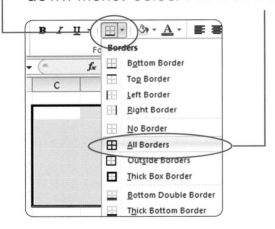

2 Now select the **Line Color** option and click on a blue to change from the default of black.

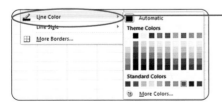

Top Tip!

All border options are on the "Border" tab of the "Font" toolset drop-down menu.

3 The **Draw table tool** appears. Click on the grid lines you want to show with blue borders or click-and-drag to draw a box.

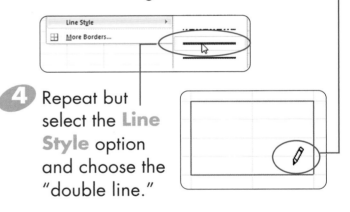

4 Repeat but select the **Line Style** option and choose the "double line."

5 Press **Esc** to stop the **Draw table tool**.

6 Select an area, then click the **Borders** button. Your selected area will have borders with the last line style and color used.

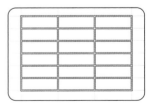

PROJECT 3 REVISION PLAN

Get your revision organized

Use a spreadsheet to create your plan

The grid layout of spreadsheets is great for setting out a quick plan.

USING IT

Remember!

Use **Esc** to stop the table drawing tool after you have changed a border setting.

 1 Open a new workbook and save it as *Revision Timetable*.

2 Set out your plan with your subjects across the top and the dates up until your exams down the side.

	English	Math	Science
1-Mar			
2-Mar			
3-Mar			
4-Mar			
5-Mar			
6-Mar			
7-Mar			
8-Mar			
9-Mar			
10-Mar			

3 Select all your table and use the **Borders** drop-down menu to set "All Borders" to thin black lines.

	English	Mat		Right Border
1-Mar				No Border
2-Mar			⊞	All Borders
3-Mar				Outside Borders
4-Mar				Thick Box Border

4 Change the line color to blue and give the plan a thick outline.

	English	Mat		Right Bord
1-Mar				No Bord
2-Mar			⊞	All Border

	English	Math	Science	French	Spanish
1-Mar					
2-Mar					
3-Mar					
4-Mar					
5-Mar					
6-Mar					
7-Mar					
8-Mar					
9-Mar					
10-Mar					

 5 Select the subjects and click the **Borders** button. Repeat for the dates.

6 Save your work.

Make cells stand out

Change cell Background Colors

HOW TO DO IT

Color cell backgrounds to make them stand out.

1 Click on a range of cells in a spreadsheet.

2 Click the **Fill Color** button on the **Home** tab.

3 The cells' background color becomes default yellow.

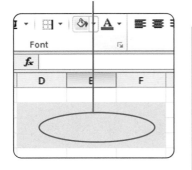

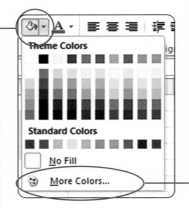

4 Click the **Fill Color** button drop-down menu to get more colors.

5 Select a new color. It will be used next time you click the **Fill Color** button.

6 Select **More Colors** to see the "Colors" dialog box and select a shade different to the "Theme Colors" or "Standard Colors."

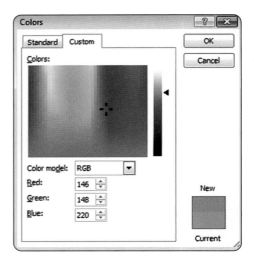

Top Tip!

You can select different cell ranges together by pressing the **Ctrl** key while selecting.

PROJECT 3 REVISION PLAN

Use color to code your plan

Color is a great way to identify something quickly

USING IT

Splashes of color break up your plan so that you can quickly see what you need to do.

1 Mark on the plan when your tests are.

2 Select a test, and click on the "Fill Color" button drop-down menu to make the fill color red.

3 Change the font color in the cell to *white bold* so that you can read it.

4 Change the fill color to a custom pale yellow and block out the days on which you're unable to revise.

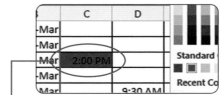

Top Tip!

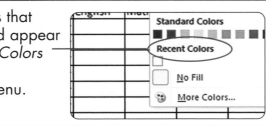

Custom colors that you have used appear in the *Recent Colors* section of the drop-down menu.

Styling cells

Use **Styles** to change the format of a cell

Styles are easy-to-apply preset combinations of fonts and alignments.

1 Click the **Cell Styles** button drop-down menu in the "Styles" toolset on the **Home** tab to see all available styles.

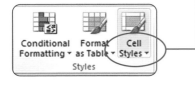

2 Select a style. This will be applied to all selected cells.

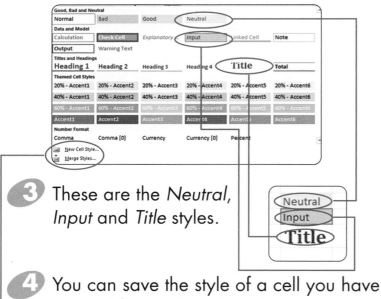

3 These are the *Neutral*, *Input* and *Title* styles.

4 You can save the style of a cell you have created for use later by selecting the **New Cell Style** option.

5 Give your new style the name *Franky 18* in the "Style" dialog box that opens up and then click **OK**.

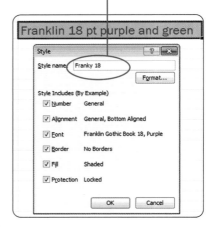

6 You can now apply your saved style from the "Custom" section of the **Cell Styles** drop-down menu.

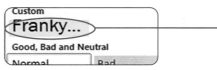

PROJECT 3 REVISION PLAN

Apply cell styles to your revision plan

Apply and create styles in your revision plan

Using styles allows you to color code your plan very quickly.

1 Give your plan a title. **Merge & Center** it across the plan and use **Cell Style** *Heading 1*.

3 Call the new style *Test Day*.

2 Select the cell you filled in red for your first test and then click on **New Cell Style** in the **Cell Style** drop-down menu.

4 Press the **Ctrl** key and then select the other tests. Apply your custom style.

Styling tables

Use **Table Styles** for quick, good-looking tables

HOW TO DO IT

"Table Styles" are a quick way to create good looking tables. They also add useful sort and calculation functions.

1 Select your fruit list.

2 Click the **Format as Table** button on the **Home** tab.

3 Select a style option.

4 The "Create Table" dialog box appears. Tick the "My table has headers" box and click **OK**.

5 Your table now looks great. If it also has headers, each one will have a "Sort" drop-down menu button too. Click on them to sort your lists automatically.

Notice also that the **Table Tools – Design** tab has appeared on the ribbon.

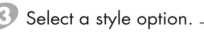

PROJECT 3 REVISION PLAN

Style your plan with a table style

Using a table style will give your plan a professional feel

Applying a table style will make your plan really smart.

 Select the whole revision plan.

 Click the **Format as Table** button and apply a table style.

 The cells that you have already formatted will keep their style, but the rest will take the new one.

4 Hover-over different table styles to preview how they would look.

More table style options

Add **Total** and **Header Rows**

HOW TO DO IT

What do the new drop-down menu buttons at the top do? Adding a "Total Row" is an easy way to add up columns.

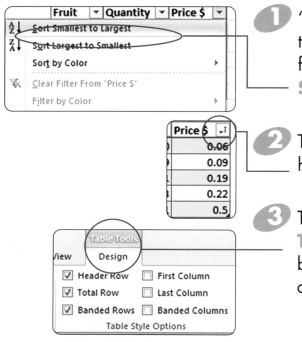

1 "Sort" drop-down menu buttons were added to the header row of the fruit list when it was formatted. Click the *Price* column one and select **Sort Smallest to Largest**.

2 The list is now sorted by price. Notice the button has changed to show this.

3 Tick the "Total Row" checkbox on the **Table Tools – Design** tab. A new row is added at the bottom of the table and the final column is added up.

4 Click on the **Total** cell for the *Price* column. A drop-down menu button appears. Click the button to view the options.

5 Select **Sum** to get the total for the column or **Average** to get the average for the column.

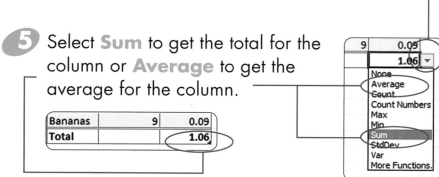

Top Tip!

To get rid of the "Sort" drop-down menu buttons in the heading cells, click the **Convert to Range** button in the "Tools" toolset.

Tools

PROJECT 3 REVISION PLAN

Apply some table style options

The table style options can also be useful for your plan

By using the built-in table tools we can help organize the plan.

1 Insert a column before every subject and reduce the width to 25 pixels.

2 Start planning your revision. Put how many hours you are going to do on a subject in the small column. Increase the row and column sizes and use **Wrap Text** if necessary.

3 Select the **Total Row** option from the **Table Tools – Design** tab.

4 Use the **Sum** option in the Total Row, to work out how much time you are giving to each subject. Use **Count** for each subject to see how often you are revising it.

Top Tip!

Use the cell style to clear other cell styles you have applied.

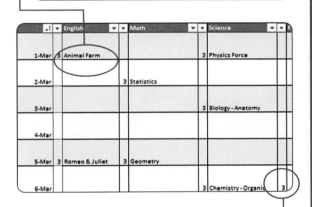

Challenge!

"Sort" and "Unsort" your subject columns to make sure you have covered everything. "Sort Oldest to Newest" to return the table to normal.

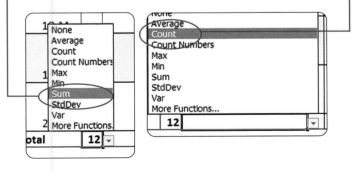

What will it look like on paper?

Using **Print Preview**

HOW TO DO IT

"Print Preview" lets you to check your work before you print it.

1 Create a spreadsheet named *Holiday Plan*. Make a table starting in cell **C5** with three very wide columns, 15 tall rows and a title. Apply a "Table Style" to the cells.

2 Click on the **File** tab and then the **Print** option.

3 Two new areas are displayed: the **Print** area and the **Print Preview** area. Your spreadsheet will be shown as it will appear on paper.

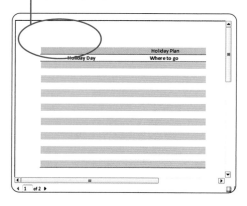

You can get to the **Print** area by selecting **Print Preview and Print** in the "Quick Access" toolbar. If you don"t see the option, click on the drop-down menu and select it.

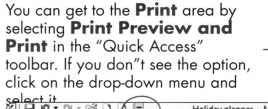

4 The "page turner" at the bottom left of the **Print Preview** area allows you to see what it will look like on each page.

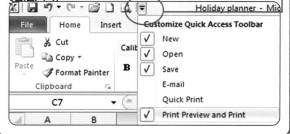

5 At the bottom right, the **Zoom to Page** tool allows you to preview the entire spreadsheet, while the **Show Margins** tool shows where your spreadsheet will start printing from.

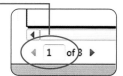

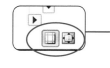

6 Press **Esc** or click on the **Home** tab to return to the normal view. Notice the dotted lines now on screen. These outline each printed page.

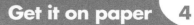
PROJECT 3 REVISION PLAN

Get ready to print

What will your plan look like on paper?

Print your revision plan so you can have it for easy reference.

1 Open your *Revision Plan 1* workbook.

2 Open it in the **Print Preview** area.

3 Use "Zoom to Page" and the "page turner" to view it completely.

4 Save your work and then save it as *Revision Plan Small*.

5 Change column, row and font sizes until the plan fits onto one page. Preview as you do this to check progress.

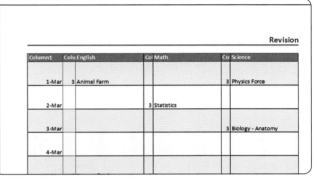

Print part of your work

The **Print Area** tool

HOW TO DO IT

Excel will print everything from cell **A1** to the last row and last column where you have edited a cell. To print just a part of your spreadsheet you need to set the "Print Area."

1 Select the part of your work that you want to print.

2 Click the **Page Layout** tab on the ribbon and then select the **Print Area** button.

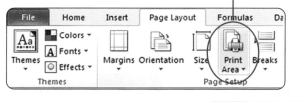

3 From the drop-down menu, select **Set Print Area**. ————

4 A dotted line appears around your selection and inside if your **Print Area** will print on more than one page.

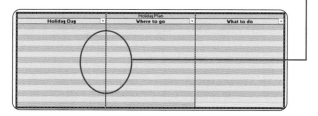

5 Once you have set the **Print Area**, the **Add to Print Area** option appears in the drop-down menu allowing you to print several selected areas at once.

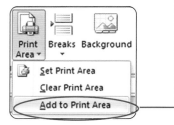

6 Click on **Clear Print Area** to return to printing the entire spreadsheet.

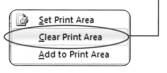

PROJECT 3 REVISION PLAN

Print just the table

Set the print area for your plan

Excel sets margins on your paper automatically; you don't need the blank columns and rows.

1 Open *Revision Plan 1* again and insert four rows and two columns.

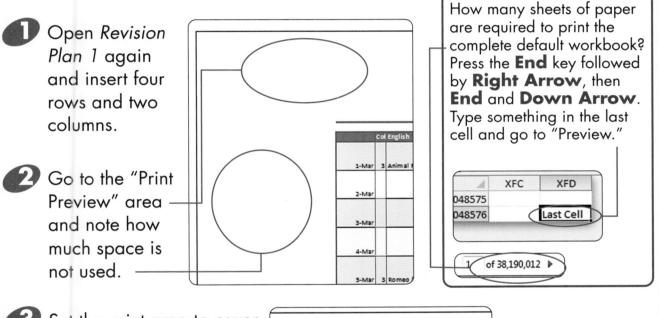

2 Go to the "Print Preview" area and note how much space is not used.

3 Set the print area to cover the entire plan and preview it again.

4 There will still be white areas above and left, but these are the standard margins. There will be fewer pages required.

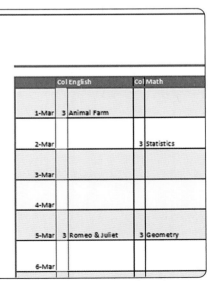

	Col English		Col Math
1-Mar	3	Animal Farm	
2-Mar			3 Statistics
3-Mar			
4-Mar			
5-Mar	3	Romeo & Juliet	3 Geometry
6-Mar			

The long or the wide of it

You can print with your paper landscape or portrait

HOW TO DO IT

Tables are often wider than they are tall, so are better printed as "Landscape" rather than the default of "Portrait."

1 In the *Holiday Plan* spreadsheet go to the **Print** area on the **File** tab.

2 In the "Settings" section, you will see the "Orientation" setting currently set to **Portrait Orientation**.

Settings

Print Active Sheets — Only print the active sheets		▾
Pages: ⬍ to ⬍		
Print One Sided — Only print on one side of the page		▾
Collated — 1,2,3 1,2,3 1,2,3		▾
Portrait Orientation		▾
Legal — 8.5" x 14"		▾
Normal Margins — Left: 0.7" Right: 0.7"		▾
No Scaling — 100 Print sheets at their actual size		▾

Page Setup

Top Tip!

A painting of a *landscape* is usually wider than it is tall, while a *portrait* is taller than it is wide.

3 Click on this to see and select the **Landscape Orientation** option.

Portrait Orientation ▾
Portrait Orientation
Landscape Orientation

4 The **Print Preview** area will be updated to show the new layout.

Holiday Plan
Holiday Day   Where to go

PROJECT 3 REVISION PLAN

Which way is best for the plan?

Change the orientation setting to preview in landscape

The revision plan needs to be printed as efficiently as possible.

1 Set the revision plan to landscape.

2 Check the result in the **Print Preview** area.

3 Change it back to portrait and compare the two options.

4 Decide which is best, then save your spreadsheet.

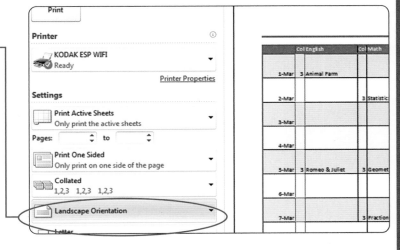

Top Tip!

More print settings are available from the **Page Layout** tab. The "Page Setup" toolset dialog box is available from the ribbon or the settings area.

Page Setup

Excel has tools to optimize printing

Use the **Scaling** settings to make your spreadsheet to fit your paper

HOW TO DO IT

You can manually change your spreadsheet to fit or you can use scaling settings.

1 In the **Print** area settings, the default scaling option is "No Scaling."

Settings

| Print Active Sheets |
| Only print the active sheets |

Pages: [ ] to [ ]

| Print One Sided |
| Only print on one side of the page |

| Collated |
| 1,2,3   1,2,3   1,2,3 |

| Portrait Orientation |

| Legal |
| 8.5" x 14" |

| Normal Margins |
| Left: 0.7"   Right: 0.7" |

| No Scaling |
| 100 Print sheets at their actual size |

2 Select **Fit Sheet on One Page** if you want your spreadsheet on just one sheet of paper.

3 The **Print Preview** area will allow you to see if the scaling has made your work illegible.

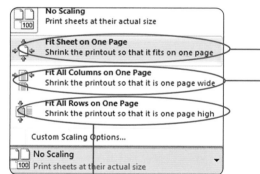

| No Scaling |
| 100 Print sheets at their actual size |

| Fit Sheet on One Page |
| Shrink the printout so that it fits on one page |

| Fit All Columns on One Page |
| Shrink the printout so that it is one page wide |

| Fit All Rows on One Page |
| Shrink the printout so that it is one page high |

Custom Scaling Options...

| No Scaling |
| 100 Print sheets at their actual size |

Holiday Plan

| Holiday Day | Where to go | What to do |

4 If you have a very long table, try **Fit All Columns on One Page** or, if it is wide, try **Fit All Rows on One Page**. You may need to change the orientation if you use these options.

Top Tip!

Use the **Narrow** margin setting to maximize the printed area.

PROJECT 3 REVISION PLAN

Fit your plan for printing

Fit your plan to make it fit your purpose

Experiment with scaling options for your revision plan so that you can use it on paper.

1 Open the *Revision Plan 1* and go to the "File" tab.

2 Set the scaling to **Fit Sheet on One Page**. Check the preview. Change the orientation if necessary.

3 Set the scaling to **Fit All Columns on One Page** then **Fit All Rows on One Page**.

4 Select your best combination and save your workbook.

Top Tip!

It can be quite easy to make mistakes when doing the finishing adjustments to your spreadsheet. The **Versions** section of the **Info** area can help you revert.

Manage Versions ▾

Versions

📄 Today, 10:01 PM (autosave)
📄 Today, 9:49 PM (autosave)
📄 Today, 9:37 PM (autosave)
📄 Today, 9:23 PM (autosave)

Info

Print your document

The **Print** and **Quick Print** buttons

HOW TO DO IT

Once you are sure your spreadsheet is ready, go ahead and print.

 Go to the **Print** area of the "File" tab.

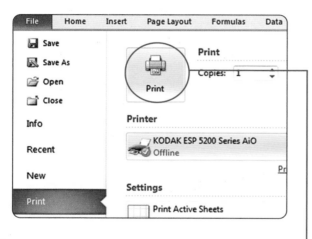

 If you want to print more than one copy, type in the number of copies, or click on the **Up Arrow** until you get the right number.

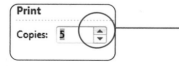

3 Click on the **Print** button to print your work.

4 You can also print a single copy by clicking on the **Quick Print** option in the "Quick Access" tool bar.

PROJECT 3 REVISION PLAN

Let's print the plan

We should now be ready to print!

Having checked the settings, we are ready to print.

USING IT

1 Use **Quick Print** from the "Quick Access" toolbar to print your planner.

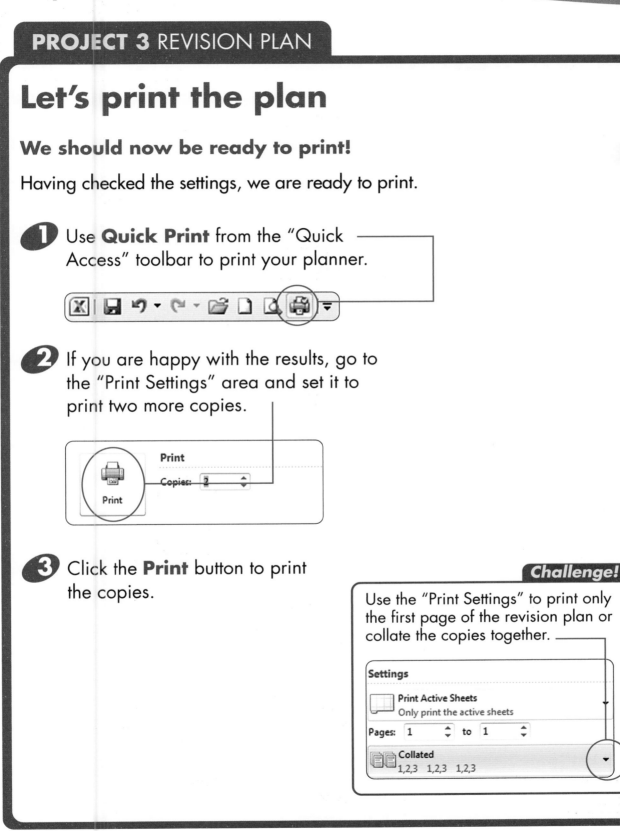

2 If you are happy with the results, go to the "Print Settings" area and set it to print two more copies.

Print

Copies: 2

Print

3 Click the **Print** button to print the copies.

Challenge!

Use the "Print Settings" to print only the first page of the revision plan or collate the copies together.

Settings

Print Active Sheets
Only print the active sheets

Pages: 1 ⇅ to 1 ⇅

Collated
1,2,3 1,2,3 1,2,3

5 Speeding things up

Copy and paste

Remember!

Use "hover-over" to learn more about the buttons on the ribbon.

Repeat something without having to retype it

HOW TO DO IT

You often need to copy things again and again on spreadsheets.

1 Select the "source" cell(s) you want to copy.

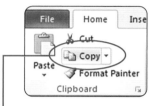

2 Click the **Copy** button on the **Home** tab. The cells are highlighted with a moving dotted line.

3 Click the "destination" cell you want to copy <u>to</u>. If you have copied several cells, this will become the top left cell of the range.

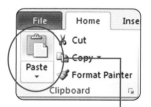

4 Click the **Paste** button. A copy of the source cell is now in the "destination" cell. To copy again, select another "destination" cell and again click **Paste**.

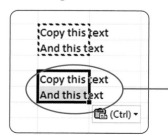

5 You can repeat pasting as long as the "source" cell(s) are still highlighted.

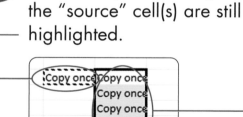
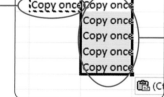

6 You can paste a single cell into several "destination" cells. Each one is filled with a copy of the "source" cell when you click **Paste**.

Top Tip!

You can paste what you copy into other programs such as Outlook or Word. Use **Copy as Picture** if you want to make sure it looks the same.

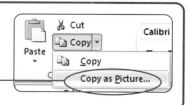

56

Create a diary by building up blocks

Use copy and paste to build up a large spreadsheet

USING IT

Duplicate monthly planning tables to build up a calendar.

1 Save a new spreadsheet as *My Diary*.

2 In cell **C5** start a table with days of the month to 31 across the top and times of day down the side. Style it appropriately.

3 Select your table and click **Copy**.

4 Select a blank cell in column **C** and click **Paste**.

5 Select both your tables and click **Copy**.

6 Select another blank cell in column **C** and click **Paste**.

7 Repeat until you have 12 tables.

Moving

Move things around the spreadsheet

HOW TO DO IT

Moving or cutting and pasting content helps you to reorganize your work.

 Select the cells you want to move.

 Click the **Cut** button on the **Home** tab.

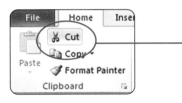

 The cells are highlighted with a moving dotted line.

◢	B	C	D	E	F
14					
15		Move this from here			
16					
17					
18				to here	
19					

4 Click on the "destination" cell the cut cells must move <u>to</u>.

5 Click the **Paste** button. The cut cells disappear and reappear at the "destination" cell.

6 To move cells directly, select them and hover-over the edge of the selected area until the mouse pointer changes to crossed arrows.

Move this from here

7 Click-and-drag the cells to a new position.

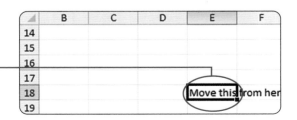

◢	B	C	D	E	F
14					
15					
16					
17					
18				Move this from her	
19					

PROJECT 4 MY DIARY

Move your diary

Use cut and paste to rearrange things

USING IT

Cut and paste allows you to place the diary where you want it.

 Select the first row of the diary.

 Cut and paste it into cell **A3**.

3 Select the other rows and cut and paste them below the first one.

 Select the next table and click-and-drag it to column **A**.

5 Move all the remaining tables to column **A**.

6 Save your spreadsheet.

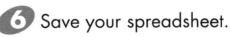

Turn back time

Using the **Undo** and **Redo** buttons

HOW TO DO IT

You will sometimes make mistakes and need to reverse them.

1 Open a workbook and select a cell. Apply the *Good* style to it.

2 Click the **Undo** button in the **Quick Access** toolbar. The style will disappear.

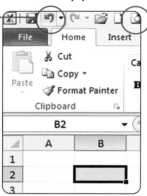

3 Type the numbers *1* to *6* in column **C**.

4 Click the **Undo** button drop-down menu to see a list of recent actions – in this case, typing numbers into cells. Click **Typing "3" in C3**. Everything up to that is undone and only *1* and *2* remain.

5 If you have undone too much, click the **Redo** button until you get back to where you want, or click the drop-down menu and select the actions you want to redo.

PROJECT 4 MY DIARY

Put it back where you found it

Use Undo to reverse your changes

USING IT

On second thoughts, the diary was fine the way it was!

1 Undo the pastes that moved the table from its original position.

3 Select a large block of your table and press the **Delete** key.

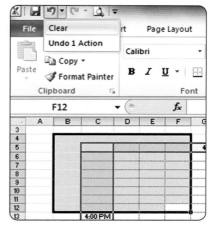

2 Redo the pastes to get the tables back to their positions starting in cell **A3**.

4 That was a big mistake! Undo it.

Top Tip!

The keyboard shortcut for undo is **Ctrl** + **Z**. This is a standard shortcut for most PC programs.

The history of copying

Using the Clipboard

HOW TO DO IT

Every time you "copy" or "cut" something it is added to the
Clipboard for reuse.

 Click the **Clipboard** toolset drop-
down menu on the **Home** tab.

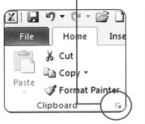

 The **Clipboard** appears showing
recently copied "Clips."

3 To reuse a "Clip," select a
destination cell then select the
desired "Clip" on the **Clipboard**. It
gets pasted to your selected cell(s).

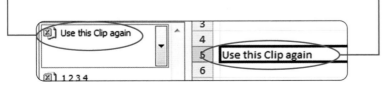

4 The **Clipboard** holds 24
"Clips." New "clips" replace the
oldest ones. To keep an older
"Clip," delete newer ones by
hovering-over a "Clip," clicking
its drop-down menu button and
selecting **Delete**.

5 To close the **Clipboard**, click
the **Close** button in the top right
corner of it.

Top Tip!

The "Clipboard" holds
information from other
programs too. Great if
you are copying from a
Word document!

The Clipboard speeds this next part up

A cheat to generate month headers

USING IT

By using **Auto Fill** and the **Clipboard** you can save time with repetitive tasks.

1 Insert a new worksheet in front of the *My Diary* worksheet. Call it *Diary Cover*.

2 In a cell type *January* and below, *February*. Use **Auto Fill** to create 12 months.

3 Format the months using the *Header 2* style.

4 Open the **Clipboard**. Click on each month and then click the **Copy** button.

5 Click back on the *My Diary* worksheet and insert a column in front of column **A**.

6 Starting next to the top block, click on *January*, then move down to click on *February* and so on.

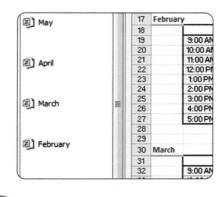

7 Close the **Clipboard**.

Copy just the value

Copy, but keep the format of where you are pasting

HOW TO DO IT

The **Paste** button drop-down menu has several useful options. **Paste Values** allows you to paste the <u>content</u> of a cell without its <u>style</u>.

 1 In a worksheet, type into cells as below. Give two cells a yellow background and 14pt blue font with a red dotted border. Make the backgrounds of the other two cells green with font 24pt *Book Antiqua*.

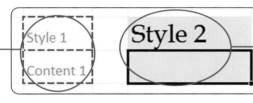

2 Copy a *Style 1* cell. Select the empty *Style 2* cell. Pasting into this gives it a *Style 1* style.

 **3** To avoid this, click the **Paste** button drop-down menu and select **Paste Values**.

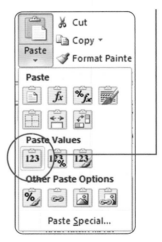

4 The <u>content</u> (the text) but not the <u>formatting</u> (the style) has now been pasted.

Top Tip!

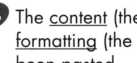

You can also do this after you have pasted by clicking on the **Paste Options** button and selecting the **Paste Values** option.

Inserting into the diary without affecting the font

USING IT

Work out your key dates, then use Paste Special

Write a list of events then paste them into the diary using **Paste Special**.

1 Set the body of your diary to 9pt with **Wrap Text**.

2 In your *Diary Cover* worksheet type out a list of special events.

Special Events
My birthday
Dad's birthday
Mom's birthday
Christmas
Thanksgiving
Easter
Halloween
Mother's day
New Year's day

3 Copy the events one by one onto the **Clipboard**. Then use **Paste Values** to paste them into your diary. If you don't use **Paste Values**, the grid lines will be deleted.

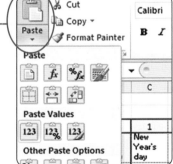

4 Save your diary.

Top Tip!

You can add the "Paste Gallery" (drop-down menu of Paste options) to the **Quick Access** toolbar. Right-click on it and select "Add Gallery to Quick Access Toolbar."

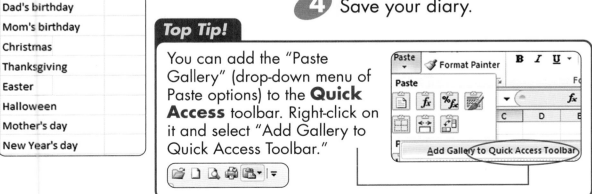

Copy just the style

The **Format Painter**

HOW TO DO IT

Sometimes you want to copy just the <u>style</u> of a cell, not the content.

1 Click on the cell whose style you want to copy.

			Cut	Book Antiqua	24
	Copy			B I U	
Paste	Format Painter				
	Clipboard			Font	

	F5			fx	Style 2
	D	E		F	
1					
2					
3					
4					
5	Style 1			Style 2	

2 Click the **Format Painter** button from the "Clipboard" toolset.

3 The mouse pointer will change to a paintbrush icon to show that the "Format Painter" is active.

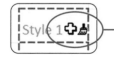

4 Click or click-and-drag over the cells you want to apply this styling to. This paints the source cell style onto the destination cells.

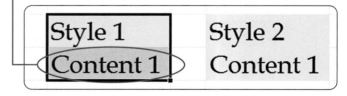

Style 1	Style 2
Content 1	Content 1

5 The "Format Painter" is only available once. Click back on the source cell and repeat to use it again.

Style your key dates

The Format Painter will help you to be consistent

USING IT

The "Format Painter" can be used to copy a special style for your key dates.

1 Click on one of your special events. Change the background color to orange and increase the font size to 10pt.

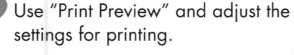

2 Use the **Format Painter** to apply the style to the entire day.

3 Use the **Format Painter** to apply the style to other days.

4 Use "Print Preview" and adjust the settings for printing.

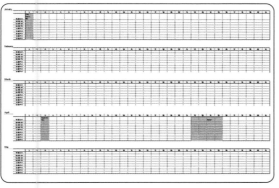

Challenge!

Use "Page Breaks" from the "Page Setup" toolset to make sure a month is not printed over two sheets of paper.

Linking together

Using **Hyperlink** to get about

HOW TO DO IT

You can use hyperlinks like those on the internet to move quickly around a spreadsheet.

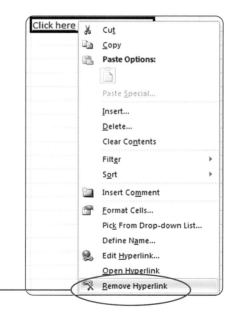

1 Type *Jump to here* in a cell on a worksheet and *Click here* in another cell in a different worksheet.

2 Select the *Jump to here* (destination) cell. In the "Name Box," type the name *Link1.* (Names can't have spaces in them.)

3 Click on *Click here* (link) cell. Click the **Hyperlink** button on the **Insert** tab. The "Insert Hyperlink" dialog box appears.

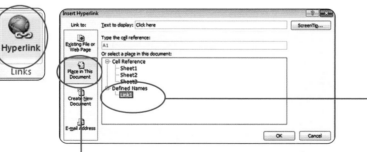

4 Click the **Place in This Document** button and select the name (*Link1*) from the "Defined Names" list. Click **OK**. Note the cell style has changed to *Hyperlink*.

Click here

5 Clicking on the link cell will move you to the named destination cell. Right-clicking on the source cell will let you select the **Remove Hyperlink** option.

Get around your diary

Add links from the months on the *Diary Cover*

The diary is a very large document. Links from the front cover will make it easy to get to the right month.

 Select each month cell in the *My Diary* worksheet and name it.

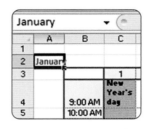

2 Go to the *Diary Cover* worksheet and select *January*. Add a hyperlink to the defined name *January*.

3 Repeat for the other months.

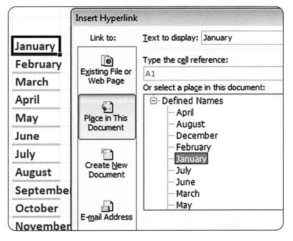

4 Click on a link to take you to that month.

5 Notice that links change color once used. This is automatic in **Excel**.

Check your text

Using the **Spellchecker** and **Thesaurus**

HOW TO DO IT

Excel can check spellings and help with language.

1 To check your spelling, click the **Spelling** button in the **Review** tab.

2 If it finds a query, the "Spelling" dialog box appears, with the problem word in the "Not in Dictionary" field.

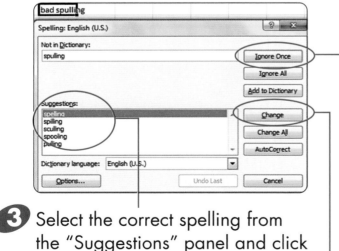

3 Select the correct spelling from the "Suggestions" panel and click **Change** or, if you are happy with the spelling, click **Ignore Once.**

4 To use the Thesaurus, click the **Thesaurus** button. The "Research" dialog box appears.

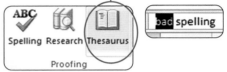

5 If you have a cell selected or a word selected in the formula bar, a list of similar words appears. Otherwise type your word in the "Search for" field and click the "Green Arrow" button.

PROJECT 4 MY DIARY

Correct and clarify

Double check your work and your vocabulary

Check your diary text.

 Open the *My Diary* worksheet.

 Select cell **A1** and click the **Spelling** button.

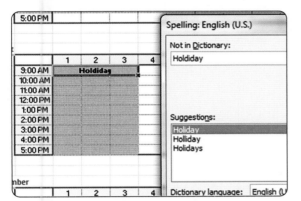

Top Tip!

Press the **F7** function key to start the spellchecker.

 Correct any errors.

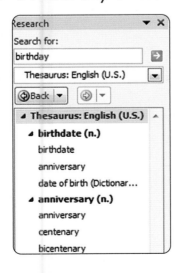

 Click the **Thesaurus** button.

 Find a new word for *Birthday*.

 Save and close the *My Diary* spreadsheet.

Simple sums

Simple calculations in a cell

HOW TO DO IT

Excel is designed to do number crunching, from simple to very difficult calculations.

 Any calculation in **Excel** begins with =. This tells **Excel** that the cell contains a calculation, not text.

 To add two numbers, click in a cell and type =10+10. Then press the **Enter** key.

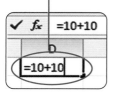

 The answer, *20*, is shown in the cell, while the calculation is shown in the formula bar.

4 To subtract, use the – key. Multiply is * and divide is /.

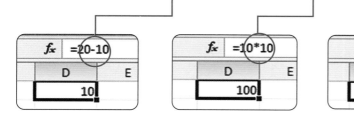

PROJECT 5 CLASS SURVEY

Class statistics

Adding, subtracting, dividing and multiplying

The class survey project demonstrates basic math skills. Learn to use **Excel** like a calculator first. It will be easier to do the more difficult stuff later.

 Save a spreadsheet as *Class Survey*.

 Type *Name* in cell **A3** and add the class"s names to column **A**.

G	H	I	J	K
		Travel to School		
Name	Distance (mls)	Time (mins)	Time (hrs)	Speed (mph)
Michael	1.2	15		
Felix	0.5	10		
Sophie	0.3	5		
Ali	3.2	10		
Kinga	2.5	15		

3 In cells **B3** to **E3** type *Cats, Dogs, Other,* and *Total*.

▲	A	B	C	D	E
1					
2			Number of Pets		
3	Name	Cats	Dogs	Other	Total
4	Michael				
5	Felix				
6	Sophie				
7	Ali				
8	Kinga				
9					

4 **Merge & Center** the cells in row 2 and add a title *Number of Pets*.

5 Copy the table to cell G2 and change the headers to *Distance (mls), Time (mins), Time (hrs),* and *Speed (mph)*. Give it the title *Travel to School*.

6 Complete the *Number of Pets, Distance,* and *Time (mins)* columns.

Name	Cats	Dogs	Other	Total
Michael		1	2	3
Felix		2	0	1
Sophie		0	1	0
Ali		0	0	1
Kinga		0	2	0

 In cell **E4** add up the number of pets that Michael has.

Name	Cats	Dogs	Other	Total
Michael		1	2	3 =1+2+3
Felix		2	0	1

8 In cell **J4** calculate the time, in hours, that Michael takes to get to school.

Name	Distance (mls)	Time (mins)	Time (hrs)	S
Michael	1.2	15	=15/60	

Start the power

Simple calculations between cells

HOW TO DO IT

You can also do calculations <u>on</u> the numbers in cells. For example, you can add up the contents of five cells and put the answer in a sixth cell.

 Open a new spreadsheet and name it *Calculation*.

 Type the numbers *43, 56, 345, 67* and *65* into cells **D2** to **D6**. We will now add these up and put the answer in cell **D7**.

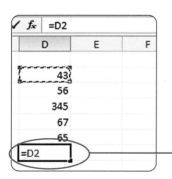

3 In cell **D7** (our answer cell) type **=**, then click on cell **D2** containing the first number. *D2* appears (not the number inside it) meaning the calculation will be done using the number contained in cell **D2**.

 Press the **+** key and then click the next cell. Repeat for all the cells with numbers. Cell **D7** will show *=D2+D3+D4+D5+D6*.

✓ f_x	=D2+D3+D4+D5+D6	
D	**E**	**F**
43		
56		
345		
67		
65		
=D2+D3+D4+D5+D6		

5 Press the **Enter** key to tell **Excel** the calculation is complete. The answer cell **D7** now shows the result of adding the contents of the five cells together (*576*).

6 Change the number in **D3** from *56* to *0*. Notice the number in the answer cell has changed to *520*. The calculation is updated automatically.

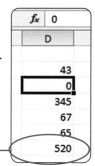

PROJECT 5 CLASS SURVEY

Add, subtract, multiply, and divide your data

Replace simple calculations with cell references

Using cell references means it's easy to change calculations when numbers change.

 Change the calculation in cell **E4** for Michael's total number of pets to use cell references.

Name	Cats	Dogs	Other	Total
		Number of Pets		
Michael	1	2	3	=B4+C4+D4
Felix	2	0	1	

> **Remember!**
>
> The column letter and row number of a cell are called the <u>Cell Reference</u>. Cell **A1** is the top left cell of a worksheet.

 Do this for each class member.

Name	Cats	Dogs	Other	Total
Michael	1	2	3	6
Felix	2	0	1	3
Sophie	0	1	0	1
Ali	0	0	1	1
Kinga	0	2	0	=B8+C8+D8

 Change Michael's school travel time to use cell references. The time in minutes is in cell **I4** here.

Name	Distance (mls)	Time (mins)	Time (hrs)
Michael	1.2	15	=I4/60

4 Calculate Michael's speed in mph by dividing the distance (**H4**) by the time in hours (**J4**).

Name	Distance (mls)	Time (mins)	Time (hrs)	Speed (mph)
Michael	1.2	15	0.25	=H4/J4

5 Save your work.

Build up steam

Copying formulas

HOW TO DO IT

People who use **Excel** in their jobs can fill a spreadsheet with calculations. It's easy when you learn how to copy calculations.

 1 Create two columns numbered 1 to 10.

 2 Create a formula to multiply the first two numbers together.

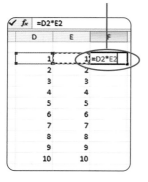

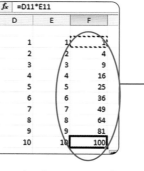

3 Copy the cell with the calculation and paste it into the cells below. **Excel** automatically adjusts the cell references. See how the first row shows =D2*E2. **Excel** has adjusted the next row so the calculation is =D3*E3.

4 You may want to copy cells without this happening. In this example, we want to show how many British pounds and Swiss francs we get for

US dollars as the exchange rates change. Cell **D4** contains the exchange rate for pounds, so the calculation for $5.00 worth of pounds in cell **D5** is =C5*D4.

If this formula is copied to cell **D6** it becomes =C6*D5 with a result of 31 when it should be 6.20.

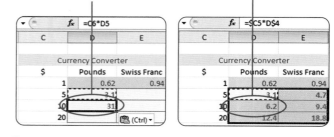

5 To tell **Excel** to copy a formula <u>without</u> the cell reference being adjusted, you must add the $ symbol to the <u>column</u> and/or <u>row</u> reference. In the *Currency Converter* example, we change the formula in cell **D5** to =$C5*D$4.

Complete the calculation columns

Copy formulas to finish the survey

USING IT

Complete the survey by copying the formulas.

 1 Select cells **J4** and **K4** containing the time (hrs) and speed (mph) calculations.

Travel to School				
Name	Distance (mls)	Time (mins)	Time (hrs)	Speed (mph)
Michael	1.2	15	0.25	4.8

2 Click **Copy**, then select from cell **J5** to the bottom of your table.

Travel to School				
Name	Distance (mls)	Time (mins)	Time (hrs)	Speed (mph)
Michael	1.2	15	0.25	4.8
Felix	0.5	10		
Sophie	0.3	5		
Ali	3.2	10		
Kinga	2.5	15		

3 Click **Paste**. All the calculations for the class have now been done.

Time (hrs)	Speed (mph)
0.25	4.8
0.1666667	3
0.0833333	3.6
0.1666667	19.2
0.25	10

 4 There are 5,280 feet in a mile and 3,600 seconds in an hour. In cell **L2** type *=5280/3600*.

5 Type *Speed (ft/s)* into cell **L3**. Calculate the speed in <u>ft/s</u> for Michael in cell **L4** using the ratio calculated in **L2**.

hool			1.4666667	Conversion Factor
s)	Time (hrs)	Speed (mph)	Speed (ft/s)	
5	0.25	5	=K4*L2	

6 Edit the formula to stop the reference to cell **L2** being adjusted when the calculation is copied.

		1.4666667	Conversion Factor
	Speed (mph)	Speed (ft/s)	
5	5	=K4*$L$2	

7 Copy cell **L4** to the rest of the class.

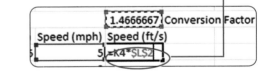

	1.4666667	Conversion Factor
Speed (mph)	Speed (ft/s)	
5	7.3333333	
3	4.4	
4	5.8666667	
19	27.866667	
10	14.666667	

Total power

Adding up using **AutoSum**

HOW TO DO IT

Excel can add cells together easily using "AutoSum."
This adds the numbers in selected cells together and
puts the answer in a cell.

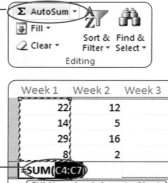

 Open a new spreadsheet and copy the
example table.

 Click on cell **C8** in the "Total" row.
Click the **AutoSum** button on the
Home tab.

 AutoSum guesses what cells you want
to add together. Press the **Enter** key if
correct, otherwise click-and-drag to
select the correct cells and press the
Enter key. The sum of all the cells
appears in **C9**.

4 Alternatively, type =*Sum(* into a cell, click-and-drag to
select the cells you want added, then press the **Enter**
key. Again the sum appears.

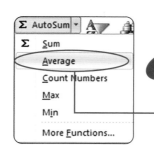

5 Other AutoSum options are available in the **AutoSum**
button drop-down menu. Click on cell **G4** and then select
Average from the **AutoSum** button drop-down menu.
This will give you the average score for *Player 1*.

Use AutoSum with your survey

Change the total row to use AutoSum

We can use AutoSum to add *Total* and *Average* rows to the survey.

1 Type *Total* below the last name in the *Number of Pets* table.

2		Number of Pets			
3	Name	Cats	Dogs	Other	Total
4	Michael	1	2	3	6
5	Felix	2	0	1	3
6	Sophie	0	1	0	1
7	Ali	0	0	1	1
8	Kinga	0	2	0	2
9	Total				

2 Use AutoSum to calculate the total number of cats in the class. Click on the cell below the *Cats* column and then click the **AutoSum** button.

Name	Cats	Dogs	Other
Michael	1	2	3
Felix	2	0	1
Sophie	0	1	0
Ali	0	0	1
Kinga	0	2	0
Total	=SUM(B4:B8)		

SUM(**number1**, [number2], ...)

3 Copy and paste this cell to the *Dogs, Other* and *Total* columns.

Total		3	5	5	13

4 Type *Average* in the cell below the last name in the *Travel to School* table. Click on the cell below the *Distance (mls)* column and use AutoSum to calculate the average distance.

	Travel to School		
Name	Distance (mls)	Time (mins)	Time (hrs)
Michael	1.2	15	0.25
Felix	0.5	10	0.1666667
Sophie	0.3	5	0.0833333
Ali	3.2	10	0.1666667
Kinga	2.5	15	0.25
Average	=AVERAGE(H4:H8		

AVERAGE(**number1**, [number2], ...)

5 Type the *=Average(* formula to get the average time [mins]).

2.5	15	0.25
1.54	=AVERAGE(I4:I8	

AVERAGE(**number1**, [number2], ...)

6 Save your work.

Mathematical methods

Formulas and functions

Inserting functions into a spreadsheet

HOW TO DO IT

There are hundreds of functions like *=Today()* in **Excel**. Each produces an answer from the numbers you put in. You will probably never need to use most of them, but you should know how to find and use them.

1 Most functions are in the "Function Library" toolset on the **Formulas** tab.

2 Click the **Logical** button to see common "Logical Functions."

3 "IF" is the most useful logical function. It gives different answers depending on whether something is <u>true</u> or not. For example, we can show if a player's score is above or below a team average.

4 Insert a new column in front of column **E**. Name it *Week 2 Av*. In cell **E8** calculate the average for *Week 2* (*=AVERAGE(D4:D7)*).

5 Click on cell **E4**, then click the **Logical Function** button and select the **IF** option. The "Function Arguments" dialog box opens.

6 Write *D4>E8* in the **Logical_test** field (is *Player 1*'s score higher than average?), "*Above*" in the **Value_if_true** field and "*Below*" in the **Value_if_false** field. "*Above*" is shown in **E4** as the answer is *Yes*.

PROJECT 5 CLASS SURVEY

Using the logical function IF

We can use IF to build up our surveys

USING IT

Excel functions are often used to analyze information. Let's use the "IF" function in our class survey to discover some things about the students' pets.

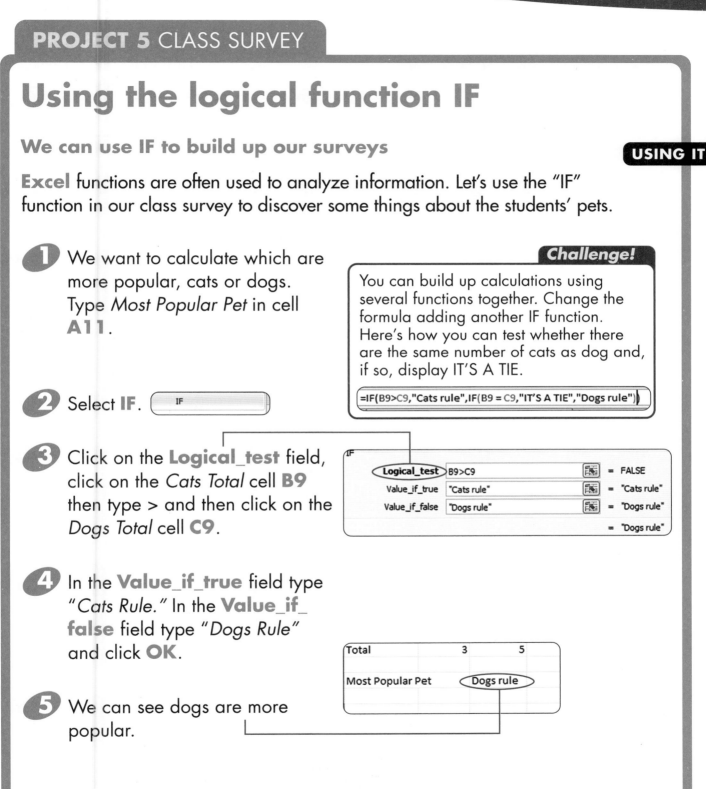

1 We want to calculate which are more popular, cats or dogs. Type *Most Popular Pet* in cell **A11**.

Challenge!

You can build up calculations using several functions together. Change the formula adding another IF function. Here's how you can test whether there are the same number of cats as dog and, if so, display IT'S A TIE.

=IF(B9>C9,"Cats rule",IF(B9 = C9,"IT'S A TIE","Dogs rule"))

2 Select **IF**.　IF

3 Click on the **Logical_test** field, click on the *Cats Total* cell **B9** then type > and then click on the *Dogs Total* cell **C9**.

IF			
Logical_test	B9>C9		= FALSE
Value_if_true	"Cats rule"		= "Cats rule"
Value_if_false	"Dogs rule"		= "Dogs rule"
			= "Dogs rule"

4 In the **Value_if_true** field type *"Cats Rule."* In the **Value_if_false** field type *"Dogs Rule"* and click **OK**.

Total	3	5
Most Popular Pet	Dogs rule	

5 We can see dogs are more popular.

Making a point

Fixing the number of decimal places

> **Remember!**
> Use the $ symbol to fix cell reference when using functions. Don't use the **Round** results in further calculations. You'll get mistakes.

HOW TO DO IT

Rounding numbers up or down can make them easier to read and understand.

1 To use "Math & Trig" functions, click on a cell and select an option from the **Math & Trig** button drop-down menu.

2 The **ROUND** function is one of the simplest.

3 It rounds up a number by the decimal places you tell it to. In this example, three Year 10 students did a test. The average score was 14.66667. (44/3). Calculate this in cell **D10**.

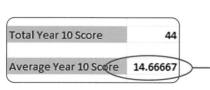

4 Click on cell **D12** and select **ROUND**.

5 In the "Function Arguments" dialog box, put *D10* in the "Number" field (the cell whose value you want to round up). Type the number of decimal places needed in the "Num_digits" field. *0* rounds to the nearest whole number. *1* would round to the nearest 0.1 of a number.

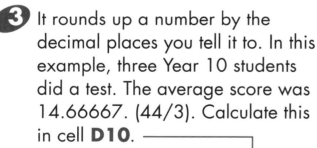

6 Cell **D12** will now show the average score to the nearest point.

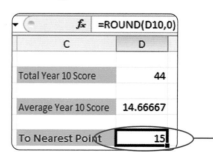

> **Top Tip!**
> If you want to round a number to the nearest 100 or 1000 you use *–2* or *–3* as the "Num_digits" argument.

PROJECT 5 CLASS SURVEY

Use the **ROUND** function

Round up our calculations to make them neater

USING IT

Some of our calculations have results with lots of decimal places. Use the **ROUND** function to tidy up the tables.

1 In the *Travel to School* table, use the **ROUND** function to round the speeds to the nearest mile per hour.

Travel to School				
Name	Distance (mls)	Time (mins)	Time (hrs)	Speed (mph) S
Michael	1.2	15	0.25	=H4/J4
Felix	0.5	10	0.1666667	3

2 Click on cell **K4**, the first mph calculation, and select the **ROUND** function.

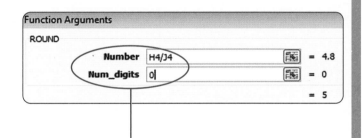

Function Arguments
ROUND
Number   H4/J4   = 4.8
Num_digits   0   = 0
   = 5

3 In the "Number" field add *H4/J4*, the original calculation in the cell. In the "Num_digits" field type *0* then click **OK**.

4 Copy this formula to the rest of the column.

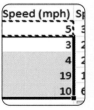

Speed (mph)	Sp
5	3
3	2
4	2
19	1
10	6

5 Repeat for the ft/s column. This time the "Number" field formula is *K4/$L$2*.

Function Arguments
ROUND
Number   K4/$L$2   = 3.125
Num_digits   0   = 0
   = 3

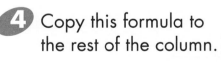

	1.466667 Conversion	
peed (mph)	Speed (ft/s)	
5	3	
3	2	
4	3	
19	13	
10	7	

Number and number

Other number formats

HOW TO DO IT

Excel normally displays up to nine decimal places, but you can increase, reduce or fix it.

1 If you calculate 1/3, **Excel** displays this as 0.333333333. You don't always want to show all the decimals.

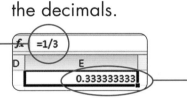

2 Click the **Decrease Decimal** button on the **Home** tab to reduce them.

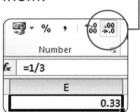

3 To increase the decimals shown, click the **Increase Decimal** button.

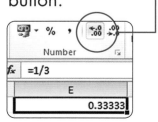

4 To <u>set</u> the number of decimal places, click the **Number Format** drop-down menu.

5 Select **More Number Formats...** and set the number of decimal places in the "Format Cells" dialog box that appears.

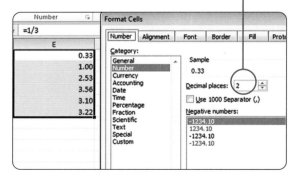

Top Tip!

To get rid of fixed decimal points, select *General* from the **Number Format** drop-down menu.

PROJECT 5 CLASS SURVEY

Tidy up the survey

Set the number of decimal places on the calculations

Some of the calculations in the class survey have too many decimal places. Fix them.

1 Set the number of decimal places in the *Distance (mls)* column to two using the **Increase Decimal** button.

G	H	I
f_x	1.2	
	Number	
		Travel to Sch
lame	Distance (mls)	Time (mins
Michael	1.2	1
elix	0.5	1
ophie	0.3	
li	3.2	

2 Set the *Time (hrs)* column to two decimal places using the "Format Cells" dialog box.

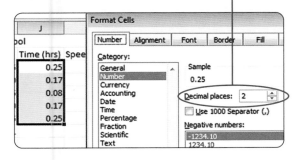

3 Use the **Decrease Decimal** button to show the average distance to school to one decimal place.

G	H	I
	Number	
f_x	=AVERAGE(H4:H8)	
G	H	I
Ali	3.20	10
Kinga	2.50	15
Average	1.5	11

4 Use the **Decrease Decimal** button to show the average speeds to the nearest *mph*.

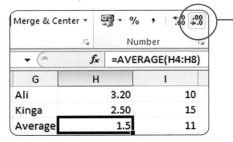

G	H	I	J	K	L
			=AVERAGE(L4:L8)		
Kinga	2.50	15	0.25	10	6
Average	1.5	11	0.18	8	5

Number and number

Other number formats: currencies, percentages and 1,000s

HOW TO DO IT

Number formats can display numbers as money, percentages and separate thousands with commas.

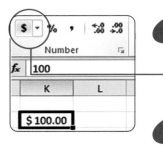

1 Show the number in a cell as currency by clicking the **Accounting Number Format** button.

2 To use another currency symbol, click the **Accounting Number Format** button drop-down menu and select one, e.g. **Euro**.

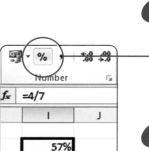

3 Click the **Percent Style** button to show numbers as a percentage where 100% = 1. So *4/7* appears as *57%* and *3.5* as *350%*.

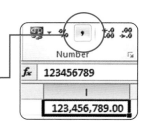

4 To show numbers with a comma separating the 1,000s, e.g. 30,000 not 30000, click the **Comma Style** button. This is a special accounting style that also fixes the cell to two decimal places.

Apply other number formats

Calculate the proportion of pets as percentages

USING IT

Percentages are a good way of showing the proportions of two numbers. Let's calculate the proportion of each pet type as a percentage.

	A	B	C	D	E
2			Number of Pets		
3	Name	Cats	Dogs	Other	Total
4	Michael	1	2	3	6
5	Felix	2	0	1	3
6	Sophie	0	1	0	1
7	Ali	0	0	1	1
8	Kinga	0	2	0	2
9	Total	3	5	5	13
10					
11	Most Popular Pet		Dogs rule		
12					
13	Percentage Pets				

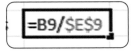 **1** In cell **A13** type *Percentage Pets*.

9	Total	3	5	5	13
10					
11	Most Popular Pet		Dogs rule		
12					
13	Percentage Pets	=B9/E9			

2 In cell **B13** divide the *Total No. of Cats* by the *Total No. of Pets*.

=B9/$E$9

3 Edit the formula to fix the cell reference to *Total No. of Pets*. Copy the formula to the *Dogs* and *Other* columns.

0.230769 | 0.3846154 | 0.384615

 4 Use the **Percent Style** button to show these fractions as percentages.

13	Percentage Pets	23%	38%	38%

87

Setting a date

Date and time formats

Top Tip!

If you type something that looks like a date, **Excel** automatically treats it as a date. So, if you type 6/6 it will show as *06-Jun*.

HOW TO DO IT

There are many ways of showing dates and times. For example, you can write *6/12/11* as *June 12th 2011* or *Sunday June 12th*. **Excel** even lets you make up your own way.

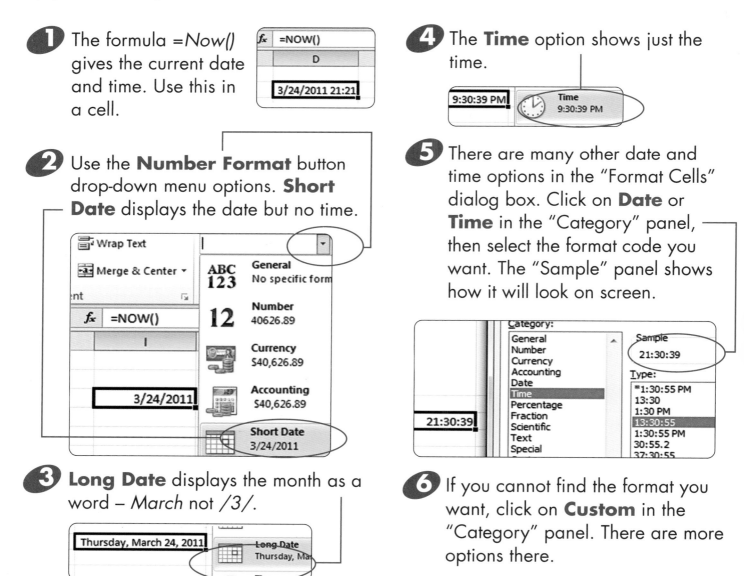

1 The formula =*Now()* gives the current date and time. Use this in a cell.

2 Use the **Number Format** button drop-down menu options. **Short Date** displays the date but no time.

3 **Long Date** displays the month as a word – *March* not */3/*.

4 The **Time** option shows just the time.

5 There are many other date and time options in the "Format Cells" dialog box. Click on **Date** or **Time** in the "Category" panel, then select the format code you want. The "Sample" panel shows how it will look on screen.

6 If you cannot find the format you want, click on **Custom** in the "Category" panel. There are more options there.

PROJECT 5 CLASS SURVEY

Apply date formats

Add ages to the class survey

Long dates are easily understood, but short ones save time.

1 Copy the class names to a new worksheet, *Age Survey*.

2 Add a column *Birthday* and add the birthdays. Set as **Long Date** format.

Birthday			$36,405.00
Thursday, September 02, 1999			**Short Date** 9/2/1999
Thursday, December 09, 1999			
Tuesday, February 01, 2000			**Long Date**
Sunday, December 17, 2000			Thursday, Se
Friday, November 05, 1999			

3 Add another column, *Age*. You can subtract one date from another in **Excel** to give the number of days between. Use the function *Today()* to calculate the age of each class member.

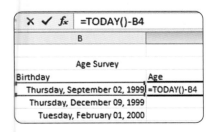

4 **Excel** will format this automatically because it's next to another long date. **Excel** dates start on Jan 1, 1900, so the age shown is from this date.

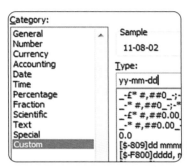

5 Select the values in the *Age* column and click on the drop-down menu in the **Number** toolset.

6 Select the "Custom" category and then in the Type field, type *yy "Years" mm "Months" dd "Days"*.

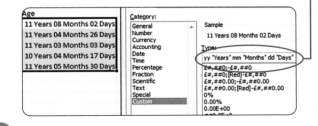

7 The class ages will now be shown in this format.

Visualize your data

Create a basic column chart

HOW TO DO IT

One of **Excel**'s strengths is the way in which it easily converts information to charts and graphs.

 Open a new spreadsheet named *Graphs* and make up a temperature table. Select the data to be turned into a graph, including headings.

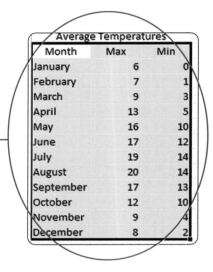

Average Temperatures		
Month	Max	Min
January	6	0
February	7	1
March	9	3
April	13	5
May	16	10
June	17	12
July	19	14
August	20	14
September	17	13
October	12	10
November	9	4
December	8	2

 Click the **Column** chart button drop-down menu on the **Insert** tab.

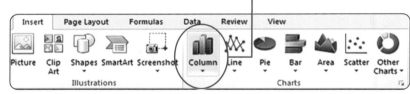

 Select a type of column chart.

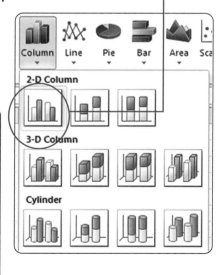

4 A new chart appears, along with the **Chart Tools** ribbon tabset.

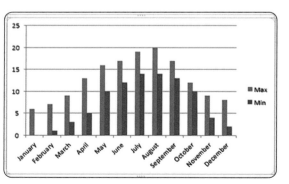

Notice how **Excel** automatically uses the first column of data for the horizontal axis and treats all other columns as data.

Top Tip!

The **Chart Tools** ribbon tabset with the **Design**, **Layout**, and **Format** tabs will reappear when you click on the chart.

PROJECT 6 CLASS PRESENTATION

Create a pet ownership chart

Use the Class Survey spreadsheet to create charts

There is lots of information in the class survey, but charts are easy to understand and they look good.

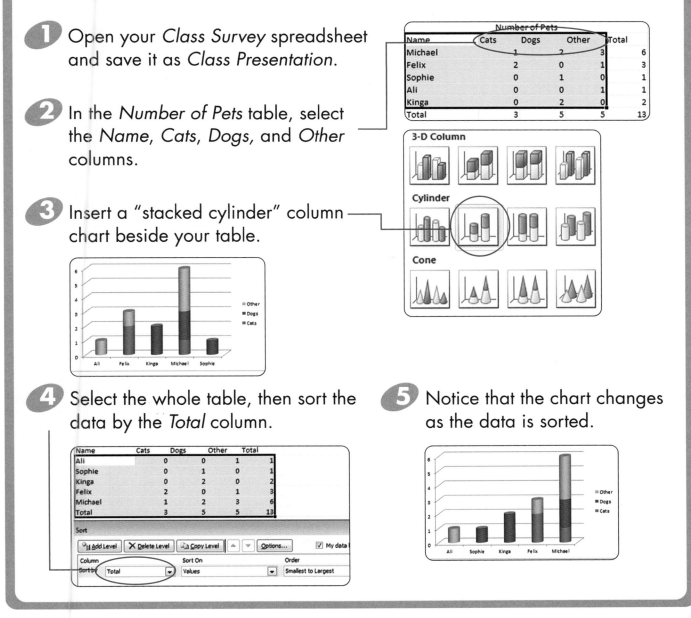

1 Open your *Class Survey* spreadsheet and save it as *Class Presentation*.

	Number of Pets			
Name	Cats	Dogs	Other	Total
Michael	1	2	3	6
Felix	2	0	1	3
Sophie	0	1	0	1
Ali	0	0	1	1
Kinga	0	2	0	2
Total	3	5	5	13

2 In the *Number of Pets* table, select the *Name*, *Cats*, *Dogs*, and *Other* columns.

3 Insert a "stacked cylinder" column chart beside your table.

4 Select the whole table, then sort the data by the *Total* column.

Name	Cats	Dogs	Other	Total
Ali	0	0	1	1
Sophie	0	1	0	1
Kinga	0	2	0	2
Felix	2	0	1	3
Michael	1	2	3	6
Total	3	5	5	13

5 Notice that the chart changes as the data is sorted.

Other ways of looking at it

Design your column chart

HOW TO DO IT

There are lots of options to adjust the look of charts in the **Design** tab of the **Chart Tools** ribbon tabset.

 1 To move your chart to another worksheet, click the **Move Chart** button.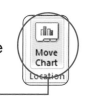

 2 The "Move Chart" dialog box appears. Either choose a worksheet or make a new worksheet. Select the **New Sheet** option, name it *Temperature Chart* and click **OK**.

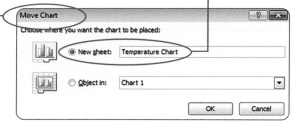

3 A new worksheet called *Temperature Chart* has been created with your chart on it.

Sheet1 ⟨ **Temperature Chart** ⟩ Chart 1 ⟨ ✍ ⟩

4 For column colors and effects, select from the "Chart Styles" toolset on the **Design** tab. Click the toolset drop-down menu to view options.

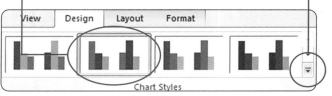

 5 Your chart will change to show the chosen style.

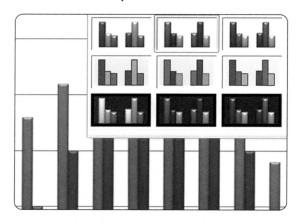

Top Tip!

Move charts around spreadsheets by clicking then click-and-dragging them into position.

PROJECT 6 CLASS PRESENTATION

Smarten up the pet chart

Use design options on the pet chart

The pet chart looks OK, but a few changes will give it real impact.

1 Move the chart to a new sheet and call it *Pet chart 1*.

2 Apply a different chart style.

3 Save your work.

Use the **Switch Row/Column** button in the "Data" toolset on the **Design** tab to make a chart showing the numbers of dogs, cats and others.

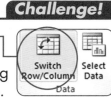

What are you looking at?

Lay out your column chart

HOW TO DO IT

The **Layout** tab on the **Chart Tools** ribbon tabset has all the options needed to label charts.

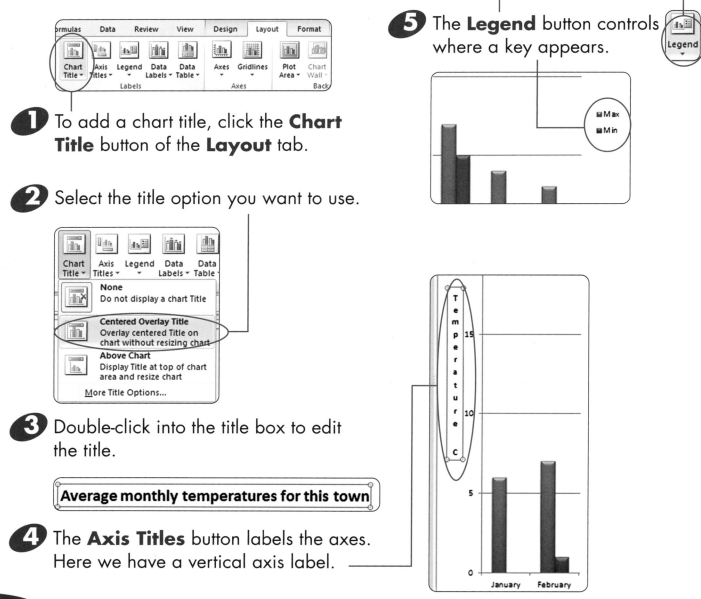

1 To add a chart title, click the **Chart Title** button of the **Layout** tab.

2 Select the title option you want to use.

3 Double-click into the title box to edit the title.

Average monthly temperatures for this town

4 The **Axis Titles** button labels the axes. Here we have a vertical axis label.

5 The **Legend** button controls where a key appears.

PROJECT 6 CLASS PRESENTATION

Select the chart layout and chart style

Add chart labels and titles

Labels help users understand what they are looking at.

1 Click on your pet chart and then the **Layout** tab.

2 Select the **Above Chart** option to add the title *Class Pet Chart* <u>above</u> it.

3 Use the **Axis Titles** button to add the vertical axis label *No. of pets.*

4 Move the legend (the key) to the left. Click-and-drag the corners to get it to sit well.

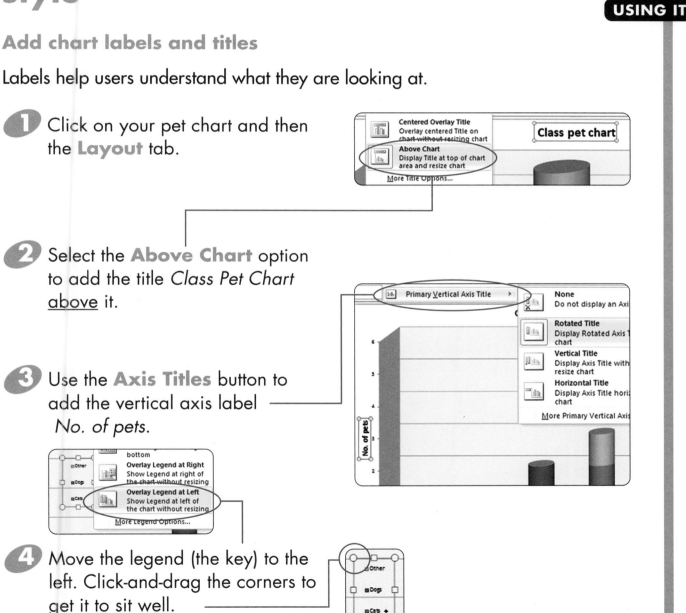

More layout options

Remember!

Click on a chart to bring up the **Chart Tools – Layout** tab options.

The **Chart Tools – Layout** tab has lots of options

HOW TO DO IT

These layout options can add information and change chart background styles.

1 The **Data Labels** button puts the actual number a column represents above or on it.

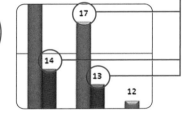

2 The **Data Table** button puts a copy of the source data on the chart – useful when the original is on a different worksheet.

3 Click the **Plot Area** button to change the chart background. Our example has a plain background so only that button is live. For 3-D look charts, **Chart Wall**, **Chart Floor** and **3-D Rotation** buttons are live instead.

4 Select **More Plot Area Options...** More Plot Area Options... for the "Format Plot Area" dialog box. Select **Fill** for options to add color, pictures or other backgrounds. Explore their effects.

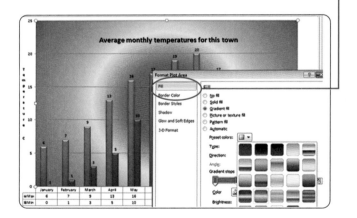

Top Tip!

The **Chart Tools – Layout** tab lets you add shapes and text boxes to a chart for comments.

PROJECT 6 CLASS PRESENTATION

Style your chart

Use the Layout tab options to add styling to your graph

USING IT

Use the **Data Labels**, **Data Table** and "Background" toolset buttons to improve your chart.

1 A stacked column chart allows only one option in the **Data Labels** button drop-down menu. Apply it.

2 Add a data table to your chart.

3 We have a 3-D look chart, so select **More Walls Options...** from the **Chart Wall** button drop-down menu and choose a "Gradient fill" for the background.

4 Do the same for the chart floor using the **Chart Floor** button drop-down menu.

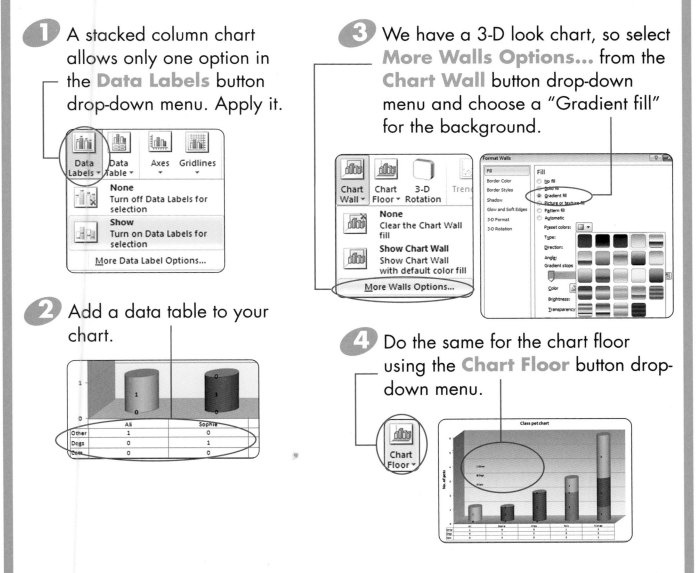

Format options

The **Chart Tools – Format** tab

The **Format** tab lets you style the text and background of different parts of your chart.

1 Click the **Format** tab in the **Chart Tools** ribbon tabset.

2 Click on the chart element you want to style, e.g. the "Chart Title." Alternatively, select it from the **Chart Elements** drop-down menu.

3 Select a "Shape Styles" toolset option to style the <u>shape</u> and <u>background</u> of the "Chart Title."

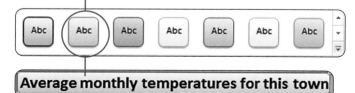

4 Style the text using "WordArt Styles" toolset options. Select the "Vertical Axis Title" from the **Chart Elements** drop-down menu and apply a style. Notice how the text changes.

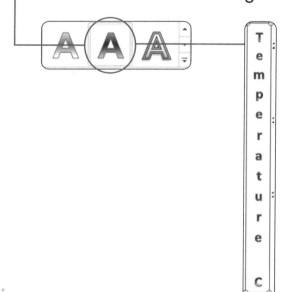

Top Tip!

These effects are fun but will look messy if you overdo them.

PROJECT 6 CLASS PRESENTATION

The final format

Use formatting on the pet chart

USING IT

Use the **Format** tab tools to improve the labels and legend of the pet chart.

1 Click the "Chart Title" and apply a shape style.

2 Click the "Legend" and apply another shape style. Click-and-drag the corners to make it bigger.

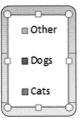

3 Click the "Vertical Axis". Apply a "WordArt" style. Select a reflection option from the **Text Effects** button drop-down menu.

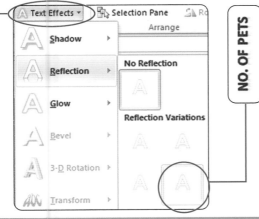

4 Increase the **Font Size** of the labels and legend using the **Grow Font** button on the **Home** tab.

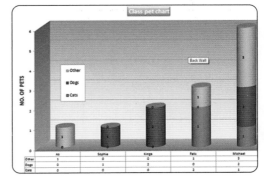

5 Save your workbook.

Challenge!

Use 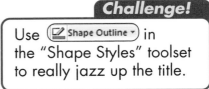 in the "Shape Styles" toolset to really jazz up the title.

Mmmmmmm, pie (charts)!

Pie charts and other chart styles

HOW TO DO IT

Excel can also create pie, donut, bar and line charts. The **Design**, **Layout** and **Format** tab options are similar to column chart ones.

1 Open a new spreadsheet and create this *Favorite Films* table. Select it.

Favorite Films	
Star Wars	12
Harry Potter 7a	22
Twilight	5
Toy Story 3	14
The King's Speech	3
Other	7

2 Click the **Pie Chart** button drop-down menu in the "Charts" toolset. Select the "Pie in 3-D" option.

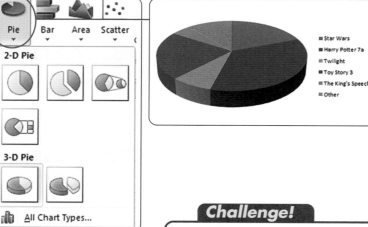

3 Click the **Other Charts** button drop-down menu and select a "Donut" chart.

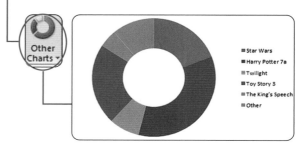

4 Bar charts are sideways column charts. Click on the **Bar Charts** button drop-down menu and select a "stacked horizontal cylinder" style.

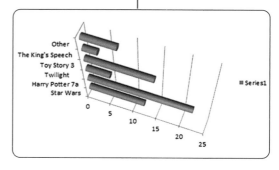

Challenge!

There are many chart types. Explore them. Where might they be useful?

PROJECT 6 CLASS PRESENTATION

A nice pet pie (chart)

Create and style a pie chart and bar chart

USING IT

Applying **Excel** charting options to the Class Survey is a great way of making the data understandable.

1 Select the *Cats*, *Dogs*, and *Other* table headings and percentages from the *Pets* table.

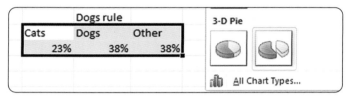

	Dogs rule	
Cats	Dogs	Other
23%	38%	38%

3-D Pie

All Chart Types...

2 Select it and make a pie chart using the "exploded pie in 3-D" style. Move the chart to a new worksheet. Format it with a chart title, data labels and large fonts.

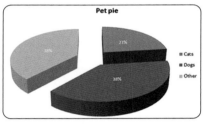

Pet pie

4 Click on the **Bar Chart** drop-down menu, and select a "Clustered Bar in 3-D" style.

3 In the *Travel to School* table, select the *Name*, *Distance* and *Time* columns.

	Travel to School		
Name	Distance (mls)	Time (mins)	T
Michael	1.20	15	
Felix	0.50	10	
Sophie	0.30	5	
Ali	3.20	10	
Kinga	2.50	15	

5 Move the bar chart to a new worksheet. Format it with a shape on the legend and a textured fill on the wall and floor backgrounds as below.

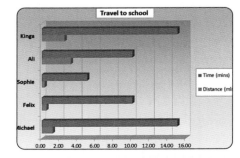

Travel to school

Adding graphics

Pictures and graphics can add interest to a spreadsheet

HOW TO DO IT

1 Click the **Picture** button on the **Insert** tab. The "Insert Picture" dialog box appears.

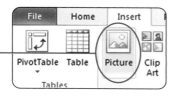

2 Find a picture on your computer, select it and click the **Insert** button. The picture appears on your worksheet.

Top Tip!

Right-click on the **Insert Picture** button to add it to the "Quick Access" toolbar.

3 The **Picture Tools – Format** tab also opens on the ribbon.

You can style it and add effects. This picture has a style that rounds off the corners and adds a reflection.

4 Specify the picture's size in the "Size" toolset or click-and-drag the corners to resize it.

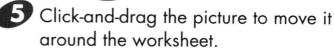

5 Click-and-drag the picture to move it around the worksheet.

PROJECT 6 CLASS PRESENTATION

A good cover page

Your presentation needs a cover page

USING IT

Use pictures to brighten up your cover sheet. With digital cameras, it couldn't be easier.

1 Add a new worksheet at the beginning of the presentation workbook.

2 Add a title, your name, and the date.

3 Add a picture of your class or school.

4 Resize the picture to 5.35 inches tall by 8.02 inches wide. Move it below your title.

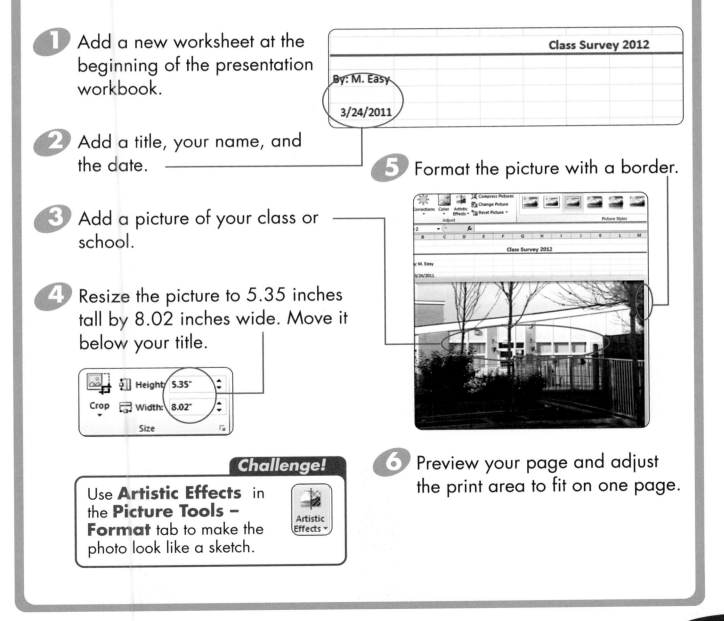

5 Format the picture with a border.

6 Preview your page and adjust the print area to fit on one page.

Challenge!

Use **Artistic Effects** in the **Picture Tools – Format** tab to make the photo look like a sketch.

Picture your PC

Use the clip tool to add a quick pic

HOW TO DO IT

Excel comes with a tool to allow you to take a quick snapshot of something on your computer.

 From the **Insert** tab select the **Illustrations** toolset and click on the **Screenshot** tool.

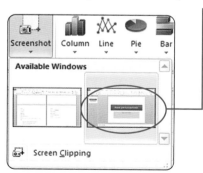

 The drop-down menu shows all the windows you have open.

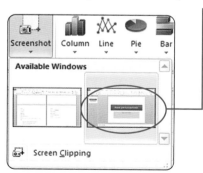

 Select the window you want and an image of it will be inserted in your worksheet.

 Select the **Screen Clipping**
 tool from the drop-down menu if you only want to capture part of the screen.

 The **Excel** window will minimize and the screen will go opaque. Click-and-drag the mouse over the area you want to capture and that image will be inserted into your worksheet.

Power point presentation

PROJECT 6 CLASS PRESENTATION

Clip from **Excel** to create an icon

Use the clip tool to illustrate your cover

Copy the graphs to your cover and jazz them up.

1 Open your school's web site.

2 Switch back to Class Presentation and click on the **Screenshot** button.

3 Click on the **Screen Clipping** button.

4 Clip the school logo from the web site.

5 Position and size it on your presentation. Give it a border style to help it fit.

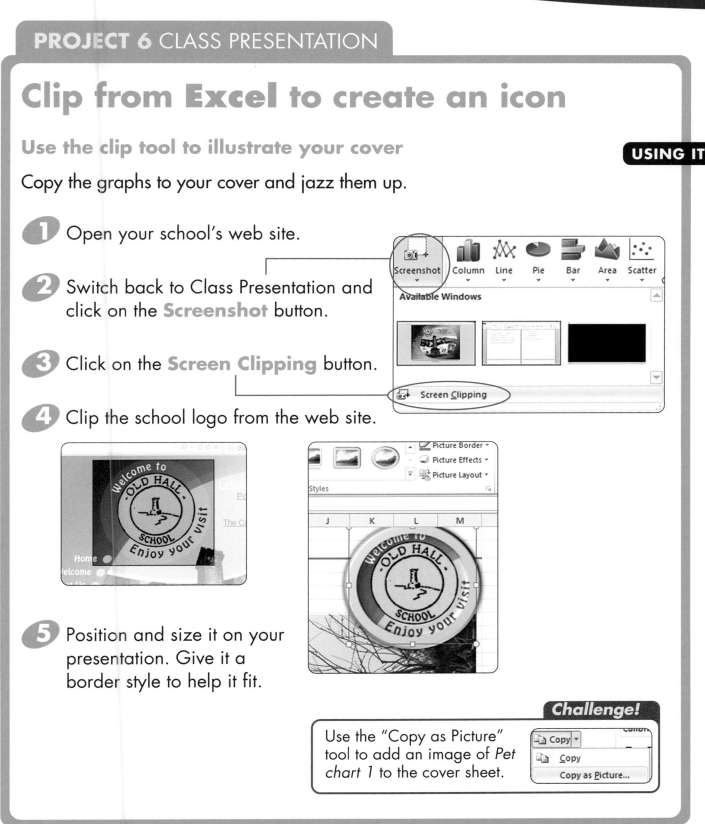

Challenge!

Use the "Copy as Picture" tool to add an image of *Pet chart 1* to the cover sheet.

105

Text effects

Using WordArt to create high-impact lettering

HOW TO DO IT

Top Tip!

You can also add "Clip Art,"
"Shapes," and "SmartArt" in
the **Illustrations** toolset.

Use "WordArt" for very noticeable text. "WordArt" can only be applied
to <u>text</u> <u>boxes</u>, not text in a cell.

1 Click the **WordArt** button drop-
down menu on the **Insert** tab.
Select a "WordArt" style.

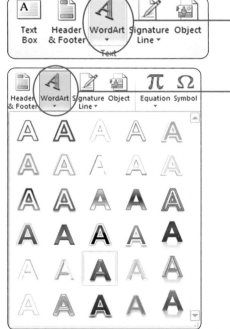

2 A text box appears containing the
words *Your Text Here*. Type over
them with your own heading *My
Excel Spreadsheet*.

3 The **Drawing Tools – Format**
tab also appears. This allows you
to style the "WordArt" even more.

4 As with charts, the **Format** tab
allows you to add some really
clever effects. This has now had a
Fill Theme and a "Perspective"
Shape Effect added from the
Shape Styles toolset.

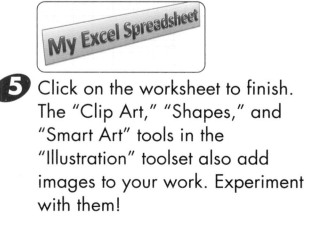

5 Click on the worksheet to finish.
The "Clip Art," "Shapes," and
"Smart Art" tools in the
"Illustration" toolset also add
images to your work. Experiment
with them!

PROJECT 6 CLASS PRESENTATION

Add a stunning heading

Use WordArt to style your heading

A bit of WordArt will have a real impact on the presentation. We'll try some 3-D effects.

1 On your cover sheet, delete the title and replace it with "WordArt."

2 Click the **Shape Effects** button drop-down menu and select **3-D Rotation**. Select one of the "Parallel" options.

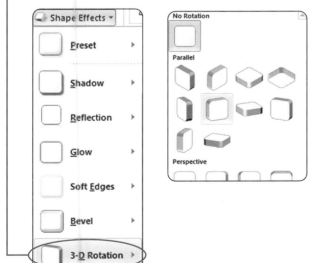

3 Adjust the positioning of the title, logo and photo. **Print Preview** to make sure it looks good on paper.

4 Save your workbook.

Print headers

Using Headers and Footers

HOW TO DO IT

"Headers" and "Footers" exist at the top and bottom of <u>every</u> printed page. They are normally empty but you can add information such as page numbers, document name or your own text.

1 Click the **Header & Footer** button on the Insert tab.

2 **The Header & Footer Tools– Design** tab opens on the ribbon and the worksheet goes to "Page Layout" mode.

3 Click into the footer or click the **Go to Footer** button to add a footer.

4 The Headers and Footers are split into Left, Right and Center areas. Click in one of these and then insert information, e.g. "Sheet Name," using the buttons in the "Header & Footer Elements" toolset.

5 These buttons add "Code Tags" into the header or footer. In this example, clicking the **Sheet Name** button adds &[TAB].

6 Click outside the header to finish editing it. The actual worksheet name, not the code tag, will be printed on every sheet.

7 Click on the "Normal" selector in the status bar to return to the usual view of the worksheet.

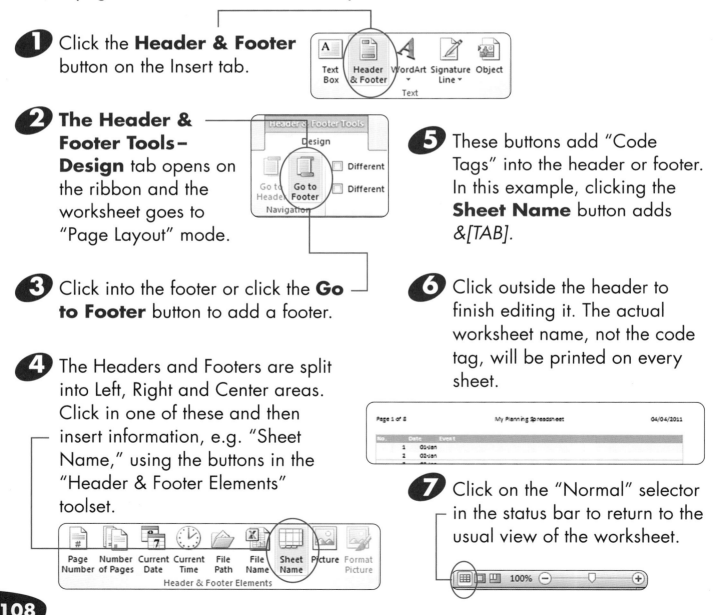

PROJECT 6 CLASS PRESENTATION

Add the worksheet title and page numbers

The class survey data pages need headers and footers.

1 Name the worksheet tab with the *Number of Pets* data on it *"Pet Survey Data."*

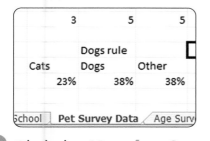

2 Click the **Header & Footer** button. Click in the left-hand section of the header and then click the **Sheet Name** button. This adds the worksheet name to every page.

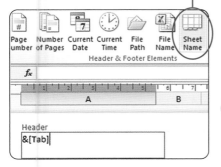

3 Insert the date in the right-hand section of the header using the **Current Date** button.

4 In the center of the footer type *Page*, then use the **Page Number** button to insert the "Page Number" code tag. Then type *of*, then insert the "Number of Pages" code tag using the **Number of Pages** button.

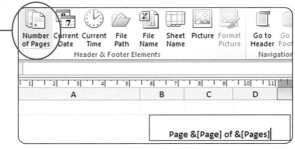

5 Check your work using **Print Preview**, and then print your table.

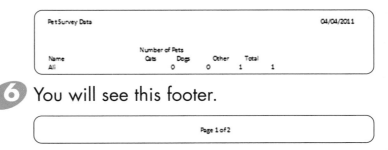

6 You will see this footer.

Page 1 of 2

Using the help menus

Other sources of help

Excel has lots of help built in. The internet has even more useful information on the subject.

1 To get "Help", click the ? icon. The "Excel Help" dialog box appears.

2 Type your query in the search field.

3 If you are not connected to the internet, **Excel** uses its built-in help.

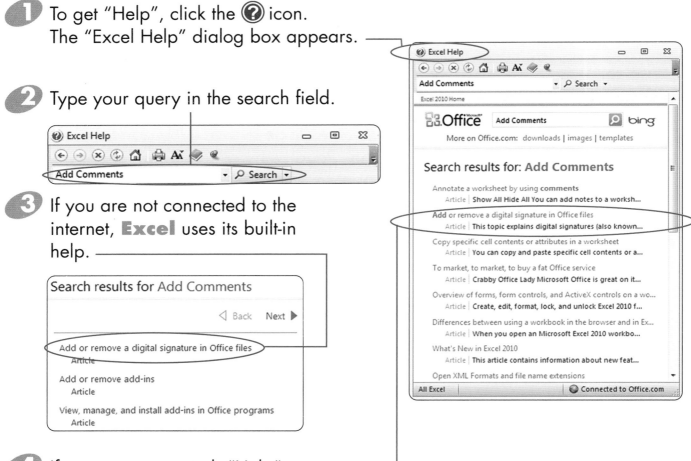

4 If you are connected, "Help" will bring back links to lots of demonstrations and videos, too.

PROJECT 7 USING THE HELP MENUS

Get yourself some help!

Did we lose you on one of the projects?

There many tools we have not had time to look at.
Use **Help** to find out about them.

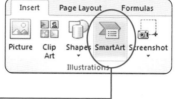

1 Search for help on "SmartArt." ——————

2 How can you add a text box? ——————

3 How do you add comments? ——————

4 How can you stop other people changing your document?

Index

fast & fun
flowers
in acrylics

fast & fun
flowers
in acrylics

LAURÉ PAILLEX

North Light Books
Cincinnati, Ohio
www.artistsnetwork.com

Published by North Light Books, an imprint of F+W Publications, Inc.,
4700 E. Galbraith Rd., Cincinnati, Ohio, 45236. (800) 289-0963. First edition.

10 09 08 07 06   5 4 3 2 1

Distributed in Canada by Fraser Direct, 100 Armstrong Avenue, Georgetown, ON, Canada L7G 5S4
Tel: (905) 877-4411

Distributed in the U.K. and Europe by David & Charles, Brunel House, Newton Abbot, Devon, TQ12 4PU,
England, Tel: (+44) 1626 323200 / Fax: (+44) 1626 323319 / Email: mail@davidandcharles.co.uk

Distributed in Australia by Capricorn Link, P.O. Box 704, S. Windsor NSW, 2756 Australia
Tel: (02) 4577-3555

Library of Congress Cataloging-in-Publication Data
Paillex, Lauré
    Fast & fun flowers in acrylics / Lauré Paillex.- - 1st ed.
        p. cm.
    Includes index.
    ISBN-13: 978-1-58180-827-8 (hardcover : alk. paper)
    ISBN-10: 1-58180-827-5 (hardcover : alk. paper)
1. Acrylic painting- -Technique. 2. Flowers in art. I. Title: Fast and fun flowers in acrylics. II. Title.
    ND1535.P35 2006
    751.4'26- -dc22
                                        2005033999

Editor: Kathy Kipp
Designer: Clare Finney
Production Coordinator: Greg Nock

Metric Conversion Chart

to convert	to	multiply by
Inches	Centimeters	2.54
Centimeters	Inches	0.4
Feet	Centimeters	30.5
Centimeters	Feet	0.03
Yards	Meters	0.9
Meters	Yards	1.1

About the Author

Lauré Paillex has enjoyed drawing and painting all her life. As a child, her love for decorative art was inspired by the Peter Hunt folk art designs painted by her mother. Although largely self-taught, she has developed her skills through independent study, diverse art courses, and associations with other professional artists. She has been teaching decorative painting for 30 years and has authored or contributed to ten instruction books, several video lessons and numerous pattern packets. Her work is regularly featured in popular decorative painting magazines and has been licensed for the gift market.

Lauré is a business member of the Society of Decorative Painters and a member of the Graphic Artist's Guild. She currently exhibits and teaches at locations around the United States and internationally as well as at her home studio, Cranberry Painter Decorative Arts, a charming antique farmhouse with saltwater and nature views of Cape Cod, Massachusetts.

Contact Information:

Lauré Paillex
P.O. Box 1495
Buzzards Bay, MA 02532-1495
Phone: 508-759-4623
E-mail: laureart@adelphia.net
Web Site: www.LaureArt.com

Dedication

My deep appreciation and thanks to the many painting friends, past and present, who have inspired, challenged and motivated me through the years. I'm especially thankful for the loving support and encouragement of my husband, Andre, to whom this book is dedicated. I am truly blessed!

Acknowledgments

I would like to thank the North Light Books team for giving me the opportunity to share my love of painting with other like-minded souls. Special thanks to my editor, Kathy Kipp, for her shared vision and her patience, to Clare Finney for the lovely layout design, and to my friend Gloria Chartier for her help in creating the delightful papercraft projects featured on the last pages. The final work is an expression of joy!

Contents

A *walk in the Maine woods* or over the salty dunes of Cape Cod, a stroll through an English garden or along an Irish hedgerow laden with late summer blackberries, or even a short trip to the local nursery or flower shop...such are the memories that became the inspiration for this book.

I've always been fascinated by flowers. As a child I had two passions. The first was being outdoors exploring and examining the tiniest details of plants and trees, using their various parts as miniatures for my doll house. The second was being indoors drawing and painting. What joy to behold a delicate flower petal created with a simple stroke of my brush! It is my hope that you will experience that same sense of delight as you combine familiar brushstrokes to create beautiful floral motifs.

The flowers presented in this book are not intended as scientific botanical studies, but as models for rendering a variety of familiar flower types. Basic acrylic painting techniques are easily mastered and a limited palette allows the creation of a rainbow of color possibilities. The step-by-step illustrations can be used as a convenient reference guide for all your floral painting projects regardless of the medium you choose.

Several bouquet, wreath, garland and border compositions are featured with patterns, but you may also use the many painted examples throughout the book as pattern ideas also. Remember to keep your pattern lines brief and simple! They are only a guide to help you visualize the general placement and shape of the floral design elements. Give your brush the freedom to create graceful petal, leaf and vine strokes. Paint with a joyful heart... always!

Introduction

"...Consider the lilies of the field, how they grow; they toil not, neither do they spin:

And yet I say unto you, that even Solomon in all his glory was not arrayed like one of these."

—Matthew 6:28-29 K. J. V.

Materials

The brushes used to paint the flowers in this book include (from left to right): rounds, liners, flats, filberts and an angular bristle. Choose the type and size that are right for the petal or leaf you are painting.

Paints

DecoArt Americana acrylic paints were used to paint the illustrations in this book (www.decoart.com). These are nontoxic, water-based acrylic paints sold in 2-ounce (59 ml) bottles. Shake the bottles well before using to make sure the binder is mixed with the pigments.

Acrylic paints can be thinned with water for strokework, linework or washes of color. There are several mediums available for thinning, blending and extending the drying time of the paint. You may wish to experiment with them. My favorite mediums are DecoArt Easy Float and JoSonja's Magic Mix. Follow the manufacturer's directions on the product label for use and techniques. Acrylic paints and mediums are available at art and craft supply stores.

Brushes

The brushes used in this book are from Loew-Cornell, Inc., 563 Chestnut Ave., Teaneck, New Jersey 07666. www.loew-cornell.com.

The series numbers used are:
#7000 – Rounds
#7350 – Short Liners
#JS-1 – Mid Liner
#7300 – Flats
#7500 – Filberts
#244 – Angular (Natural) Bristle

High quality Golden Taklon synthetic brushes are designed for painting with acrylics. With proper care, these tools will insure the quality of your work. Never let paint dry in the brush, and rinse the brush often during your painting session. Clean thoroughly with a good brush cleanser, rinse well, and return the bristles to their original shape when you're finished painting.

The Series #244 Angular Bristle is a stiff natural hair brush that can be used for stippling techniques such as foliage backgrounds and certain textured flowers, such as Queen Anne's Lace and Astilbe.

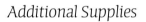

Additional Supplies

Tracing Paper – Tracing paper comes in pads or rolls in a variety of sizes and is available at art and office supply stores. Trace your design onto tracing paper with pencil or fine permanent ink art pen. Position the paper on your prepared project surface and secure along one edge with tape. Slide a piece of transfer paper under the tracing and retrace the design with a stylus.

Transfer Papers – Transfer papers are most commonly found in gray and white. A product called Blue Chaco Paper by Loew-Cornell is one of my favorites. The blue lines disappear when touched with a clean wet brush!

Stylus – This helpful tool often comes with a fine point on one end and a larger point on the other end. It is used to apply the pattern lines to your prepared surface.

Pencils and Art Pen – A supply of sharpened No. 2 pencils and chalk pencils is always helpful for sketching and tracing designs. I use a fine-point permanent ink art pen to execute the final version of a design motif.

Art Eraser – A polymer type eraser or a kneaded eraser are used to remove telltale graphite lines after the first layers of the painting are dry.

Water Basin – The Brush Tub by Loew-Cornell has three sections that can be used as a clean water source and for rinsing brushes during and after your painting session. The largest section has ribs to help vibrate the area near the brush's ferrule, making paint removal easier. Always work in one direction: upward, following the angle of the ribs. Blot the brush onto a clean paper towel to check if all the color has been removed.

Palettes – Since I like to arrange all my colors in spectrum order, I prefer to use a wet palette to keep the paints moist for long periods of time. Using a wet palette also makes it convenient to preserve my paints if my painting session is interrupted. I use a disposable dry waxed palette for all color mixing, brush loading and blending techniques.

Palette Knife – A palette knife is used for mixing two or more colors together.

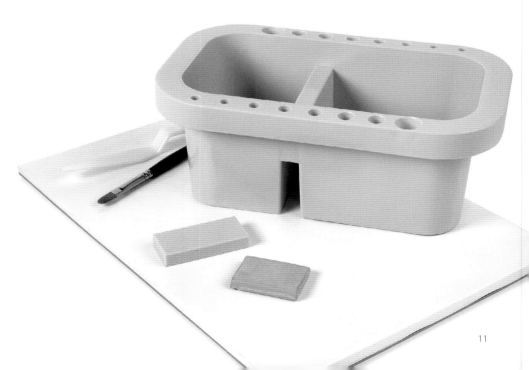

Using a Round Brush

Round brushes are identified by their round or barrel shaped ferrule, the metal tube that holds the bristles to the handle. These brushes come in many sizes and will execute a variety of strokes. Liner brushes are round brushes that have fewer yet longer bristles for creating long, flowing strokes. Select the brush size and type that best represents the size of the area you wish to paint.

1. *Basic Comma Stroke* – Beginning on the point of the brush, press, curve and lift the brush back to a point in one smooth motion forming an arc. To complete a straight stroke the brush must be rotated slightly as pressure is released to form the point.

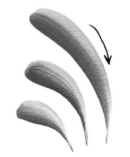

2. *Double-Loaded Comma* – Strokes may be formed with two distinct colors loaded side by side on the brush.

3. *"Thin-Thick-Thin" Stroke* – Begin with light pressure on the point of the brush and gradually press and release to form a gentle "S" curve.

4. *"Tipped" Pressure Stroke* – Load the brush with a light color and touch only the brush tip into a darker color. Begin the stroke as a small comma then apply heavy pressure, gradually lifting the brush back to a point at the end of the stroke.

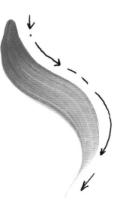

5. *"Tipped" "S" Stroke* – This stroke combines the tipped pressure stroke and the Thin-Thick-Thin to form a graceful petal shape.

6. *Dabbing* – Double-load the brush with a generous amount of paint. Use the point of the brush to dab textured dots onto the surface.

7. *Liner Brush Commas* – Press, curve and lift the brush back up onto its point as you draw it toward you. My favorite comma stroke brush is a no. 4 liner.

8. *Liner "S" Stroke* – Thin-thick-thin pressure forms graceful lines for stems, grasses and ribbons.

9. *Tendrils* - Using a liner brush fully loaded with paint thinned to the consistency of ink, glide the point of the brush across the surface forming curls and loops.

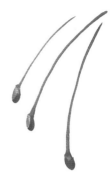

10. *Teardrops* – Begin with the point of the brush in the air above the surface and pull a curved line toward you, increasing pressure to a sudden stop at the end of the stroke.

11. *Details and Overstrokes* – Depending on the consistency and the amount of paint in the brush, one liner brush can execute a wide variety of details and embellishments.

12. *Outlining* – Use a neutral paint color thinned to a transparent wash consistency to render the initial outlines of design elements. When outlining is dry, remove any telltale graphite transfer lines with an art eraser.

Helpful Tips

- *Thin your paints* slightly with water or medium to help strokes flow smoothly and evenly from your brush. Begin with a clean brush dampened with water and blotted onto a paper towel.
- *Load the brush completely* so that the paint is fully into it about three-fourths of the way up towards the ferrule. Liner brushes may be loaded all the way to the ferrule with paint that has been thinned to an ink-like consistency.
- *Reshape the brush* before each stroke by patting it gently onto a dry palette.
- *Rinse and re-load* the brush often to avoid paint build-up in the ferrule.
- *Execute each stroke following the contour of the object* (petal, leaf, stem, etc.). Press ... curve ... lift ... carrying the stroke through in a smooth, continuous motion.
- *Use your extended little finger* for balance and support as you glide both the brush and your hand smoothly around the surface.
- *To double load a round brush,* first load one side with the lighter color, then blend the darker value into the opposite side. Set the brush onto the surface and execute the stroke so that the two colors remain distinct from each other.

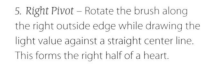

The filbert is a type of flat brush because the ferrule is crimped or flattened in order to align the bristles into a flat shape. The hairs of these brushes are set in an oval shape at the tip so that their strokes may resemble those of round brushes. They also come in many sizes and are very useful for painting flower petals and leaves.

Filbert brushes are ideal for base painting or filling in objects with curved edges. They are my favorite brushes to use for dry-brushing highlights and shadows. Larger filbert brushes with longer hairs are sometimes called "oval wash brushes."

1. *Comma Strokes* – Allow the curved shape of the brush to form the tip of the stroke. Rotate the brush onto its flat edge to form the tail of the stroke.

2. *Double-loaded Commas* – These double-loaded strokes were made with filbert brushes in size nos. 8, 4 and 2.

3. *"S" Stroke* – A double-loaded stroke is formed by gliding the brush from its knife edge to its flat side and then back to its knife edge. These strokes may face left or right.

4. *Left Pivot* – Rotate the brush along the left outside edge while drawing the light value against a straight center line. This stroke forms the left half of a heart.

5. *Right Pivot* – Rotate the brush along the right outside edge while drawing the light value against a straight center line. This forms the right half of a heart.

6. *Unfinished Strokes* – These poor little strokes have lost their tails! Execute the stroke as usual, but lift the brush from the surface leaving a dry-brushed trail where the tail should be.

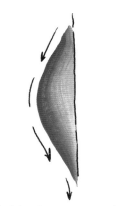

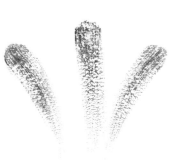

7. *Tipped Fan Strokes* – Load the brush with a light color and touch the tips of the brush hairs into a darker color. Apply heavy pressure to the brush against the surface as you fan out the bristles, then lift nearly straight up to form a variegated petal stroke.

8. *Left Slide* – Beginning on its knife edge, slide the brush along a straight line while curving the outside edge of the stroke to the left.

9. *Right Slide* – Slide the brush along a straight line while curving the outside edge of the stroke to the right.

10. *Dry-brushed Commas* – Begin with a dry brush, use undiluted paint, blot excess paint onto a dry paper towel and stroke onto a dry surface. Apply light pressure as you skim the brush across the surface in the direction of the stroke.

11. *Dry-brushed Cross-hatching* – Start with the same dry-brush method as described in Step 10. Diagonal strokes are applied in two directions for an overall softening effect.

12. *Floated Color* – Begin with a clean wet brush side-loaded along one edge with color. Pat the brush onto a dry palette to distribute the paint across the bristles until it transitions into clear water on the opposite side. Slide the color along the shaded edge of an object.

Helpful Tips

- *Thin paints slightly* and begin with a clean brush dampened with water or medium for strokework. Use undiluted paint for dry-brushing techniques.
- *Load the brush from flat side to flat side* so that it maintains its knife edge.
- *Reload the brush before each stroke* by patting it onto a dry palette.
- *Rinse and reload the brush often* to avoid paint build-up in the ferrule.
- *Execute each stroke following the contour of the object,* using the flat width of the brush to deliver the paint.
- *To double load a filbert brush,* place the lighter value on one half of the brush and the darker value next to it on the other half. Pat the loaded bristles "flat side to flat side" onto a dry palette until the colors make a gradual transition from light to dark.

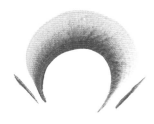

Using a Flat Brush

Flat brushes, as we have learned, are identified by a crimped ferrule which aligns the brush hairs into a flat shape with a chisel edge. This category contains such brush styles as filberts, angular shaders, wash brushes, rake/combs, fans and foliage brushes. The bristles can be of natural or synthetic fibers or a combination of both. Because they are not designed to hold a great amount of paint, you'll need a wide range of brush sizes in order to work efficiently. Always choose a brush size relative to the size of the area or stroke to be painted.

1. Simple Flat Stroke – The flat brush has a knife edge and a broad edge. The angle of the knife edge as the brush moves across the surface determines the shape of the stroke.

2. Double-loaded "S" Stroke – A double-loaded, thin-thick-thin "S" Stroke.

3. Crescent Stroke – The entire width of the brush is placed against the surface with even pressure as the stroke is formed.

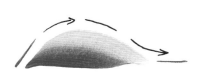

4. Upward Scroll - This stroke is pulled upward at a 45 degree angle and changes direction to form a hook at the end. A series of overlapping scroll strokes may be used to create complex leaves.

5. Simple Leaf Stroke – Use this stroke as a single double-loaded leaf or in conjunction with scroll strokes to form a fuller, multi-stroke leaf.

6. Downward Scroll – Pull the stroke downward with the brush positioned on a 45 degree angle, then change direction to form an upward hook at the end.

7. "U" Stroke – A "U" shaped motion is often used when floating shadows or highlights.

8. *Dipped Crescent* – This stroke is used to form the back and inside petals on open roses.

9. *Ruffled Petal Right* - These strokes define the individual petals on the right side of a rose.

10. *Ruffled Petal Left* – Practice this stroke with a side-loaded brush used for floated color.

11. *Floated Color* – Side load a clean, moderately wet brush, pat the brush onto your palette to diffuse the color no more than two-thirds of the way across the bristles. Place the entire width of the brush against the surface as you apply the color. The paint should transition gradually from the color-loaded edge into the clean edge.

12. *Flip Float* – Side load a clean, moderately wet brush, pat the brush onto your palette to diffuse the color no more than two-thirds of the way across the bristles. Place the color-loaded side of the brush at the center of the highlight (or shadow) and float outward, then flip your brush over and execute a mirror image of the first stroke floating in the opposite direction.

Helpful Tips

Review the notes in "Using a Filbert Brush" on page 14. These rules apply for all flat brush styles.

- *Load the brush "flat side to flat side,"* patting gently onto the palette until the loaded brush maintains a sharp knife edge along the tip.
- *Place the entire width of the brush* against the surface as you execute the stroke.
- *To side load the brush,* pick up paint on one corner of the knife edge. Pat the brush "flat side to flat side" onto the palette allowing the paint to spread no more than two-thirds of the way across the brush.
- *For floated color,* select a flat brush that is slightly larger than the area to be colored. Use clean water and thin your paints to a medium wash consistency. Side load a clean, moderately wet brush, pat the brush onto your palette to diffuse the color no more than two-thirds of the way across the bristles. Place the entire width of the brush against the surface as you apply the color. The paint should transition gradually from the color-loaded edge into the clean edge.
- *A flip float or back-to-back float* is created with a side-loaded brush dressed for floated color. Place the color-loaded side of the brush at the center of the highlight (or shadow) and float outward, then flip your brush over and execute a mirror image of the first stroke floating in the opposite direction.

Painting Terms to Know

Although the colorful step-by-step illustrations shown later in the book will show you how each flower type is developed, you'll need to be familiar with a few basic painting terms to prepare yourself for our flower painting "garden tour." With understanding and practice, you'll soon master the skills necessary for creating graceful floral studies.

There are also many wonderful books available designed to teach the basics of painting from start to finish. Some of these are listed on the final page of this book. Refer to any of them for ways to further develop your knowledge and skill.

Terms and Definitions

Basecoat – The first layer of color applied to a given area. Place color with contour-following strokes using paint that has been thinned slightly with water or medium. Use the suggested brush in the largest size appropriate for the area to be covered.

Underpainting – This refers to the manner in which color, form and texture are established in the initial stages of a painting. Undertones, highlights and shadows are placed to suggest the look and feel of the finished painting.

Sketch – A quick light outline of the basic design elements is executed using a liner or a round brush with very thin paint. Graphite transfer lines may then be safely erased before basecoating.

Dry-brush – Dry-brushing is applied in gradual layers to build up color and add texture to an area. Begin with a dry brush, use undiluted paint, blot excess paint onto a dry paper towel and stroke onto a dry surface. Apply light pressure as you skim the brush across the surface with contour-following strokes.

Diagonal dry-brush strokes are applied in two directions for an overall softening effect.

Double-load – This means to load a brush with two colors placed side by side. Blend the colors on the palette until they merge before applying the loaded brush to the painting.

Side-load – Dress the brush with clean water or medium and pull its knife edge through a puddle of fresh paint on your palette. Pat or stroke the brush onto a clean area of your palette until the paint gradually fades to clear water or medium on the opposite edge. Flat type brushes are usually used for this loading technique.

Floated Color – Side-load a flat brush with thinned paint so the paint floats across the brush from the paint side to a clear water side. Choose the largest brush that comfortably fills the area to be painted, moisten the brush with clean water or medium and blot on a damp paper towel to remove excess moisture.

Stipple – Stippling produces an airy textured effect (for flowers such as Queen Anne's Lace or for textured foliage). This may be done with an angular bristle brush. Pick up undiluted paint on the brush and fan the bristles apart on the palette. Apply the paint to the surface using a light, even, pouncing motion.

Glazing – This term generally refers to the technique of applying transparent layers of color over the completed dry painting to add unity, color balance and softness. One acrylic method is similar to a controlled watercolor technique whereby a specific area is pre-moistened with clean water before paint is applied. The moist surface will pull the color outward, causing it to fade at the edges. Sometimes layers of transparent color are applied to a dry surface using paints thinned with medium. Please follow the instructions in the individual lessons when glazing is indicated.

The Palette of Colors

The colors listed below and shown on the palette at right represent a basic "double primaries" palette, meaning that each of the primary and secondary hues has a warm and a cool variation of that color. The addition of white and three earth tones allow the flower painter to create an unlimited number of beautiful floral hues.

These colors are all DecoArt Americana acrylic paints, which were used for all the illustrations in this book.

1. *Yellow Light* – a warm, transparent yellow.
2. *Cadmium Yellow Medium* – a cool, middle value yellow.
3. *Tangelo Orange* – a warm orange.
4. *True Red* – a warm, middle value red.
5. *Santa Red* – a cool, middle value red.
6. *Napa Red* – a cool, dark red.
7. *Red Violet* – a transparent shade.
8. *Dioxazine Purple* – a dark, transparent purple.
9. *Payne's Gray* – a dark, blue-black for shading.
10. *Blue Violet* – a cool, dark value blue.
11. *True Blue* – a warm, bright blue.
12. *Evergreen* – a warm, dark green.
13. *Black Forest Green* – a cool, dark, transparent color.
14. *Olive Green* – a warm yellow-green.

15. *Warm White* – a warm, opaque white.
16. *Honey Brown* – a warm, light golden brown (raw sienna).
17. *Burnt Umber* – a dark brown.
18. *Burnt Sienna* – a warm, orange brown.

Also shown underneath the palette are the colors I used to paint all the backgrounds throughout the book. Whatever color you choose, consider adding a touch of your background color to each of your palette colors to create unity throughout the composition.

19. *Light Mocha*
20. *Hi-Lite Flesh*
21. *Light Parchment*
22. *Soft Sage*
23. *Blue Chiffon*
24. *Soft Lilac*

19   20   21   22   23   24

Using Color, Highlighting and Shading

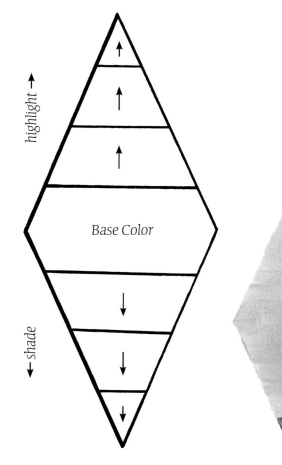

Color is the single most important factor in our floral compositions. It will be the first thing that draws the viewer's attention to your painting. Even if the strokes are not "perfect" (what petals in nature truly are?), a pleasing color scheme can exalt even the humblest blossoms.

There are many helpful resources available for the understanding and use of color: books, internet web sites, color wheels and designing tools. Take a field trip to the decorating and paint section of your local home improvement store to explore the extensive displays of paint color samples. They are helpfully arranged on individual cards by hue, value and intensity. Each of us sees and reacts to color in a unique and personal way. Start a collection of color swatches including reds, yellows, blues and neutrals that please your eye the most, and use these favorites to develop your personal palette.

In the leaf illustration above, the base color shown on leaf no. 1 represents a middle value green, which is shown in the middle of the green value scale at left. The bottom layer of the value scale is a dark value green, used for veins and shading on leaf no. 2 above. The top layer of the value scale is a light value green, which is used for the highlighting on leaf no. 3 above. The placement of the base color, the highlight colors and the shading or shadow colors on the scale gives you a visual guide as to how the layers of colors on your leaves are developed and helps you determine that all the hues are in harmony with each other.

This value scale diagram is a visual aid to show how highlights and shading are layered upon the base color. Note how each layer as you go up or down the scale covers a smaller area than the previous one. Highlights are always separated from shadows by the basecoat color. They are neither mixed with nor placed on top of each other, thus preventing colors from becoming dull, lifeless and overworked.

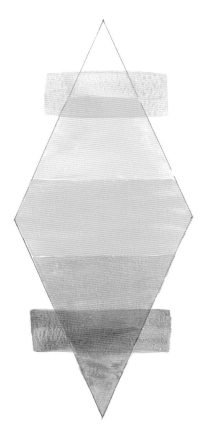

The tulip below and at right is based with a middle value yellow. Shading is developed in two steps, each darker in value than the base color. Highlights are layered with increasingly lighter values. A final glaze of transparent yellow is added to illuminate the highlights, and shadows are glazed with transparent orange. These two glazing colors are shown as extended bands on the yellow value scale at left. See pages 96-99 for tips on how to glaze colors over your flowers to achieve more richness and depth.

Here is a value scale in yellow, which was used to choose colors for the tulip at right. The base color is in the middle of the diamond-shaped scale. The highlight colors get lighter as they go up the scale to the peak of the diamond. The shading colors get darker as they progress downward toward the base of the diamond. Compare these colors to the tulip -- can you see the base color on the entire tulip? Look at the veins and shading and compare them to the base of the value scale. The lightest highlights on the tulip are at the top of the value scale.

Here the same yellow tulip is painted on a lavender background. Your flower colors will be affected by your choice of background. You may find it helpful to paint a number of 4 x 6 inch (10 x 15cm) cards in your favorite background colors as a visual reference when planning a color scheme for your flowers. Often a small amount of the background color can be added to each of your palette colors as a toner to "marry" all the elements in your composition.

Painting Leaves with a Round Brush

1.   2.   3.

1.   2.   3.

1.   2.   3.

Simple Stroke Leaf

1. Place the center vein with a liner brush. Pull double-loaded or tipped "comma" strokes inward toward the center vein.

2. Detail each stroke with fine vein lines if desired.

3. Highlight with dry-brushed overstrokes using a round or filbert brush.

Long Double-stroke Leaf

1. Place the center vein with a liner brush. Pull long, double-loaded "thin-thick-thin" strokes along each side of the center vein.

2. Detail with fine vein lines that flow with the direction of the leaf.

3. Highlight with dry-brushed overstrokes using a round or filbert brush.

Oval Double-stroke Leaf

1. Place the center vein with a liner brush. Pull double-loaded "comma" strokes along each side of the center vein, exerting enough pressure on the brush at the beginning of the stroke to fill out the width of the leaf. Keep dark color along the outside edges.

2. Detail each stroke with fine vein lines. Float dark color along one side of the center vein using a filbert or a flat brush.

3. Dry-brush highlights on the unshaded areas only.

Serrated-edge Leaf

1. Establish the center vein with a liner brush. Pull a series of double-loaded "comma" strokes outward from the center vein beginning with larger strokes at the stem end and working toward the tip of the leaf.

2. Float dark color value along both sides of the center vein, leaving the vein unshaded.

3. Dry-brush highlights in the middle of each stroke and on the center vein.

1.   *2.*   *3.*

Simple Liner-brush Leaves

1. Place the center and secondary stems with graceful linework. Pull double-loaded or tipped "thin-thick-thin" strokes outward along center vein.

2. Detail each stroke with fine vein lines if desired.

3. Dry-brush highlights using the liner brush.

1.   *2.*   *3.*

Delicate Liner-brush Leaves

1. Fine wavy lines placed with a variety of light and dark values can be used for the delicate foliage found on such plants as cosmos, ferns and dill.

2. Long, double-loaded "thin-thick-thin" strokes create graceful grasses and ribbons.

3. Delicate branches and small detail leaves are often used as filler to support the main elements in a floral composition.

1.   *2.*   *3.*

1.

2.

3.

4.

5.

Broad Flat Leaf

This is a quick and easy way to paint large leaves such as those in hydrangea and sunflower arrangements. Always choose a flat brush that is large enough to easily cover the size of the leaf.

1. Underpaint the entire leaf with light value by using overlapping scroll strokes that originate at the center vein and move outward following the contour of the leaf.

2. Add veins with a liner brush. Use the underpainting brushstrokes as a guide for the placement and direction of the veins.

3. Float shading along both sides of the center vein. Let dry. Float shading along outside edges.

4. Dry-brush highlights only on unshaded areas using a filbert brush.

5. Accent edges with floated tints of orange or red. Deepen shadows with a mix of dark green plus a touch of Payne's Gray. Brush a wash of transparent yellow over the highlights.

Multi-stroke Flat Leaf

This leaf is formed by a series of double-loaded scroll strokes that fill in the leaf area. Rotate your surface as you paint to position the leaf at the proper angle. Multi-stroke leaves make perfect companions for roses.

1. With the leaf pointing right, position the knife edge of the brush at a 45 degree angle to the center vein and fill half of the leaf with several scroll strokes ending in a point at the leaf tip. (NOTE: Left-handed painters must point the leaf to the left for this step.)

2. First half of leaf is completed.

3. Rotate the leaf so that it is pointing toward you. Fill in the opposite side of the leaf with another series of strokes. (NOTE: If you have gaps between the strokes along the center vein, you need to apply more pressure to the brush and/or use more strokes when filling in the area.)

4. Second half of leaf is completed.

5. Both sides of the leaf are properly completed. Stroke the leaf stem and center vein with a light color value using your liner brush.

6. Float shading along both sides of the center vein. Add secondary veins with a liner brush. Dry-brush highlights with white. Add transparent tints in the same manner as for the Broad Flat Leaf illustrated on the facing page. (NOTE: When several leaves overlap each other in a composition, the top-facing edges are highlighted and shading is floated along the underlying edges. See page 94 for more leaf-painting details.)

Painting Leaves with a Filbert Brush

Double-loaded Stroke Leaf

1. Place the center vein with a liner brush. Pull double-loaded strokes along the center vein keeping the dark color value to the outside edges.

2. Detail with fine vein lines. Float shading along one side of the center vein with a side-loaded filbert brush.

3. Dry-brush highlights on the unshaded areas only.

Float-shaded Leaf

1. Place the center vein with a liner brush. Base the leaf with light or medium color value using strokes that flow with the leaf shape.

2. Add vein details with a liner brush. Float shading along one side of the center vein. Let dry. Float shading along outside edges using a flat brush. Note that overlapping leaves will often require a light color value to be placed on top-facing edges.

3. Highlight with dry-brushed overstrokes.

Heart-shaped Leaf

1. Place the center vein with a liner brush. Pull double-loaded "pivot" strokes along each side of the center vein.

2. Add vein details with a liner brush. Float shading along one side of the center vein.

3. Highlight with dry-brushed overstrokes.

Serrated-edge Leaf

1. Establish the center vein with a liner brush. Pull a series of double-loaded "thin-thick-thin" strokes outward from the center vein beginning at the stem end.

2. Float dark color value along both sides of the center vein, leaving the vein unshaded.

3. Dry-brush highlights in the middle of each stroke and on the center vein. Lightly outline with dark value to unify the serrated edges.

1.

2.

3.

Multi-lobed Leaf

1. Establish the center vein with a liner brush. Pull a series of double-loaded "comma" strokes inward toward the center vein beginning at the tip of the leaf.

2. Float dark color value along one side of the center vein. Add veins and loosely outline edges with the liner brush.

3. Dry-brush highlights on unshaded areas only.

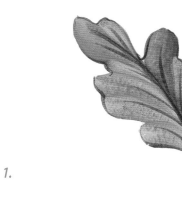

1.

2.

3.

More Filbert Brush Leaves

1. Leaves can have a translucent appearance when the paint is thinned with medium. These were rendered with a filbert double-loaded with Olive Green and Honey Brown.

2. Fine branches and delicate filler leaves can be painted in any color combination that complements your design.

3. Variations of simple strokes can produce a variety of interesting foliage such as these wavy leaves.

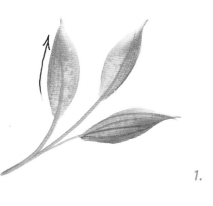

1.

2.

3.

27

What could be merrier than a rainbow of fresh summer flowers?
Use the easy step-by-step illustrations on the following pages to paint a bouquet in your favorite colors, or choose a single blossom to grace a note card or bookmark. The flowers featured in this section were chosen for their simplicity as well as their variety of size, shape and color. Explore the possibilities!

Garden Flowers

● Balloon Flower

1. Shading on petals and tip of the bud is first dry-brushed with blue violet. Stroke foliage with light value greens.

2. Place petals with filbert brush strokes using slightly thinned white.

3. Strengthen petal edges with heavier white side-loaded onto one edge of the filbert brush.

● Coreopsis

1. Each petal is placed with two or three liner brush strokes. Tap the center with light green. Stroke foliage with light and medium value greens.

2. Detail with dark color value using fine lines pulled outward from the base of each petal. Add Honey Brown pollen dots to the center.

3. Dry-brush white or light color value highlights on the petals. Tap yellow and white pollen dots on the centers.

● Viola

1. Using a filbert brush, place back petals with dark color value. Place stems and leaves with a yellow-green hue.

2. Place side petals with medium color values, double-loading the brush to create variegated strokes.

3. Front petal is placed with two strokes using a lighter color value.

4.   5.   6.

4.   5.   6.

4.   5.   6.

Balloon Flower

4. Pull detail lines from the center with light value blue. Detail the buds and foliage with medium value green.

5. Highlight petals and add final details with white.

6. Blue balloon flowers are first shaded with a mix of blue-violet plus Payne's Gray. Petals are then stroked with blue-violet.

Coreopsis

4. Coreopsis is found in several varieties and colors. Here I've painted them in yellow hues.

5. Shade and detail with Honey Brown and medium value greens.

6. Highlight with white, then accent with Yellow Light for added brilliance.

Viola

4. Add petal and leaf details using a liner brush.

5. Float-shade with dark color values to separate petals and edge leaves.

6. Paint this blue and white variety of viola following the color placement steps for the Balloon Flowers above.

Forget-Me-Nots

1. Stroke in a few directional stem lines and leaves with a double-loaded liner brush.

2. Place buds and back flower petals with medium to dark value blues using a small filbert brush.

3. Place front petals with lighter value blues.

1.   2.   3.

Hardy Primrose

1. Stroke heart-shaped petals with a filbert brush. Vary the colors to distinguish the individual petals. Base leaves and stems with Olive Green.

2. Front-facing petals are placed with lighter color values.

3. Vary the flower colors for added interest.

1.   2.   3.

Pansy

1. Place back petals with medium to dark color values using a filbert brush. Splay the bristles open at the edge of the petals and release pressure on the brush as you pull the stroke inward toward the center.

2. Place the side petals with lighter color values.

3. Place the front petal with three or four splayed strokes using the lightest color values.

1.   2.   3.

4.

5.

6.

4.

5.

6.

4.

5.

6.

● *Forget-Me-Nots*

4. Detail centers with touches of yellow and a dot of orange. Vein the leaves with dark green if desired.

5. Separate overlapping petals and add shadows with a dark blue value. Add tiny white dots around the centers.

6. Forget-Me-Nots can range in color from true blue to blue-violet to pink.

● Hardy *Primrose*

4. Pull short yellow strokes outward from the center. Add veins and loose outlines to the leaves with Evergreen using a short liner brush.

5. Float-shade a dark color value to separate petals. Shade leaves and stems with Evergreen (dark green value). Add a ring of Honey Brown pollen dots to centers.

6. Dry-brush highlights with white or a light color value. Primroses may be painted in a variety of bright colors.

● *Pansy*

4. Detail the "face" by pulling dark value strokes outward from the center using a liner brush. Center details are placed with white and yellow.

5. Separate the individual petals by float-shading with dark color values.

6. Dry-brush soft highlights with white or a light color value.

● *Cosmos*

1. Place each petal with several multi-loaded round brush strokes. Locate the flower center with Olive by dabbing with the point of the brush.

2. Vary the individual petal shapes and colors to distinguish between the separate petals.

3. Pull detail lines outward from the center with a darker color value. Use the same color to indicate the shading on the petal with the flipped edge. Tap the center with pale yellow.

4. Float-shade a dark color value at the base of each petal. Shade the indent in the center with Honey Brown.

5. Dry-brush highlights with Warm White or a very light color value.

6. Cosmos come in many bright and cheery colors. Try painting them in shades of purple highlighted with dry-brushed white or other light color value. Note that no matter what the petal color, the centers are painted the same.

Quick Tip

Cosmos are perfect for floral arrangements because they grow on long, graceful stems and have lacy, fern-like foliage. They can be painted in a rainbow of colors including pinks, yellows, violets, and white.

1.

2.

3.

4.

5.

6.

1.

3.

5.

2.

4.

6.

● Chrysanthemum

1. Lightly and loosely base the general flower size and shape with light and middle color values.

2. Establish the outer petals with round brush strokes using middle and dark color values. The back petals are longer strokes that get shorter as they come around to the front.

3. Stroke the inner petals with middle and light color values.

4. Place the front-facing petals with the lightest color strokes.

5. Shade and separate the petals with liner brush strokes. Use floated color to deepen the shading between petal layers.

6. Highlight petal tips with round brush overstrokes of white or the lightest color value. Accent the highlights with touches of transparent color washes.

❋ Quick Tips

Chrysanthemums come in so many exciting colors and varieties! If you are painting several different-colored mums in a bouquet, accent each with colors from its neighboring flower.

Leaves may be placed with filbert brush strokes. Don't forget to kiss the leaves with flower hues too!

◗ Gerbera Daisy

1. Establish flower centers and stems with Olive Green. Place back petals with round brush strokes using dark and middle color values.

2. Place remaining petals with a variety of middle and light color values.

3. Pull detail lines outward from the base of each petal using a dark color value. Begin to detail the center with mid-value green.

4. Shade the petals around the flower center with floated dark value. Detail the center with light brown pollen dots.

5. Highlight top-lying petals with dry-brushed strokes of white or lightest color value. Build pollen dot high-lights with yellow and white.

6. This is a color variation of the same flower painted with red/orange hues. After the main painting steps are completed, touches of transparent Yellow Light are added here and there to the highlighted strokes and details.

✳ Quick Tip

Leaves for daisy-type flowers may be painted with a double-loaded filbert brush using a variety of yellow-green and dark green hues. Please refer to pages 22-27 for more information about painting leaves and stems.

Zinnia

1. Place outer petals with a filbert brush using darker color values. Base leaves with Olive Green.

2. Place inner petals with mid-value colors, "tipping" the brush with a lighter color to produce streaks throughout each stroke. Apply the first shading layer along edges and center veins of leaves.

3. Establish the flower center with dark yellow and a touch of orange. Give texture to this area by dabbing the paint on with the point of a round brush. Leaf veins are painted with a liner brush using dark green value.

4. Using dark color values, pull detail lines from the center outward onto each petal and add pollen detail to the flower center. Float shading onto the base of the petals, around the center, with a flat brush using the dark color value. Develop additional shading on the leaves, such as under flower petals. Adding a touch of blue to the dark green value gives added depth to the shadows.

5. Highlight the petal tips with white that has just a hint of color added. Using the same filbert brush originally used to place the petals, tip the brush with the highlight color and pull an "unfinished" dry-brushed stroke over each petal.

6. Detail the center with yellow and white pollen dots. Add a ring of small "baby petals" around the center using the lightest color values. Accent the edges of several leaves with tints of nearby flower hues.

◗ Hollyhocks

1. Place petals with a filbert brush. Load the brush with medium value color, then touch the tip of the brush into Warm White. Splay out the bristles along the outside petal edges and release pressure on the brush as you draw the stroke into the flower center. Base the leaf and stem areas with Olive Green.

2. Float-shade the flower centers with a darker value using a flat brush. Shade leaves and stems with a mix of Evergreen plus a touch of Olive Green.

3. Detail and separate petals with White or a very light value using a liner brush. Short, irregular, wavy strokes give the impression of ruffled edges. Place the pollen centers with dots of Honey Brown and Olive Green. Dab on the long pistil with Cadmium Yellow and then highlight with White. Notice how the shape and placement of the center relates to the angle of the flower.

4. Highlight petals and leaves with dry-brushed strokes of White, reserving the brightest highlights for front-facing petals.

1.

2.

3.

4.

1.

2.

3.

● *Belladonna Delphinium*

1. Place buds and petals with brush-mixes of Blue Violet plus White using short filbert brush strokes. Stroke the leaves and stems with various yellow-green mixes using a round brush.

2. Detail the petals with Blue Violet vein lines. Shade the centers of front-facing flowers with a touch of Blue Violet plus Payne's Gray mix. Add veins, loose outlines and details to the leaves and stems with Evergreen.

3. Highlight petals and leaves with dry-brushed strokes using round or filbert brushes. Use Warm White on the petals and a mix of Warm White plus Olive Green on the leaves. Complete the centers with dots of Olive Green accented with White.

● *Geranium*

1. Establish flower stems and framework with a liner brush using middle value greens. Place outer petals and buds with filbert brush strokes using middle red values. Base leaves with Olive Green.

2. Place middle and front-facing florets with lighter red values, "tipping" the brush with the lightest value color to create natural veining in the petals. Add vein patterns to the leaves with a liner brush using dark green.

3. Highlight the centers of each front-facing floret with white liner brush strokes. Float-shade the outer edges of the leaves with a flat brush using a dark green.

4. Detail the floret centers with the middle red value. Add one or two white pollen dots to the shaded centers. Float-shade back petal edges with dark red. Detail the leaves with a pattern of layered rings, noting the flat oval shape of each leaf. Inner rings are first dry-brushed to establish shape, then overstroked with the knife edge of a filbert brush using dark green.

5. Dry-brush leaf highlights with white plus a touch of Olive. Accent the leaf highlights and floret centers with tints of Yellow Light. Tint leaf edges here and there with touches of red.

1.

2.

3.

4.

5.

❍ Sunflower

1. Place petals with a round brush using Cadmium Yellow. Blend a touch of Honey Brown into the brush occasionally to indicate shadows here and there. Fill the center with Burnt Sienna by dabbing with the point of the round brush. Base the leaf and stem areas with Olive Green.

2. Add detail lines at the base and tip of each petal with a mix of Honey Brown and Tangelo Orange using a fine liner brush. Fill in any spaces at the base of the petals with Olive Green. Add veins, loose outlines and details to the leaves and stems with Evergreen. Begin to shade the center by dabbing the edges with Burnt Umber.

3. Float-shade the underlying petal edges with Honey Brown. Shade the leaves and stems with Evergreen. Add short detail strokes of Evergreen to the spaces between the petals. Deepen the shadows on the flower center with a mix of Burnt Umber plus a little Payne's Gray.

4. Highlight petals and leaves with dry-brushed strokes using round or filbert brushes. Use Warm White on the petals and a mix of Warm White plus Olive Green on the leaves. Accent the highlights with touches of Yellow Light. Complete the center by highlighting with dabs of Tangelo Orange and Cadmium Yellow.

1.

2.

3.

4.

● *Hydrangea*

1. Loosely establish the flower's size and shape with filbert brush strokes using a middle value blue. Place stems and leaves with a middle value yellow-green hue.

2. Develop the outside petals with double-loaded filbert brush strokes using lighter and darker blues. Begin to vein the leaves with white plus a touch of yellow-green. Note the lighter color placed on the underside of the flipped edge of the leaf.

3. Place the remaining middle and front-facing petals as distinct and separate individual florets. These may be painted in lighter or darker values depending on your background or the desired effect. Outline the leaves and detail the stems and branches with darker green.

4. Outline and detail the middle and front-facing petals with liner brush strokes in white. Float-shade the leaves along both sides of the center vein with dark green.

● Hydrangea

5. Highlight front-facing florets with white floated outward from the centers. Several layers may be needed to achieve adequate brightness. Allow ample drying time between layers. Continue to layer shading values on the outside edges of the leaves.

6. Place a touch of yellow-green at the center of each highlighted floret. Float-shade outer petals and separate several inner petals with blue-violet.

7. Detail floret centers with dots of white. Add final vein lines to the leaves with dark green. Tint the deepest shadows on petals and leaves with touches of blue-violet.

8. This is a how a white hydrangea may be painted. Depending on your background color for needed contrast, establish the flower size and shape with mid-green hues. Gradually add white to the petal overstrokes and highlights. Detail and shade with green values. Finally, add kisses of pink here and there on petals and leaves for a spark of added interest.

Whether common roadside weeds or cultivated kitchen herbs, wildflower families have a naturalized beauty all their own. This collection of flowers features fine, graceful foliage and delicate blossoms that are easily rendered with a few basic brushstrokes. Keep your designs open and airy to convey a fresh, healthy, out-in-the-country feeling.

Wildflowers and Herbs

Clover

1. Place stems with a liner brush. Stroke heart-shaped leaves with a double-loaded filbert brush. Establish the flower head with a soft pink ball.

2. Add short, spiky petal strokes around the outside edges of the flower head using a small round or liner brush.

3. Fill in the center of the flower with additional overlapping strokes. Add fine detail strokes to the leaves.

Buttercups

1. Place stems and leaves with liner brush strokes using light and medium value greens. Place back petals with a filbert brush loaded with Cadmium Yellow tipped with Antique Gold.

2. Add front-facing petals with Cadmium Yellow tipped with White. Tap yellow-orange into the centers.

3. Detail the petals and centers with Antique Gold. Highlight the petals with dry-brushed white.

Thistle

1. Stroke stem framework, calyx and leaves with a liner brush using light and medium value greens. Flower heads are developed with red-violet liner strokes.

2. Detail the leaves, stem and calyx with dark value green. Build up flower strokes with red-violet plus white.

3. Detail the flower head near the center with dots of white. Dry-brush foliage highlights with Olive Green.

1.

2.

3.

1.

2.

3.

1.

2.

3.

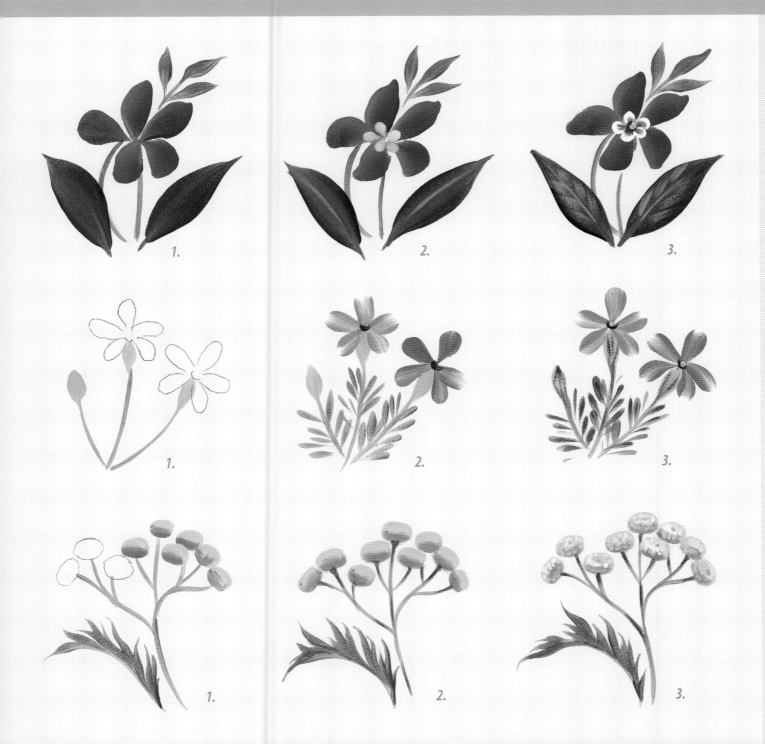

Periwinkle

1. Place petals with double-loaded filbert brush strokes using light and medium blue-violet values. Stems and small leaves are yellow-green, and mature leaves are dark green.

2. Place a small white petal at the base of each large petal. Detail leaf veins with yellow-green.

3. Detail the small center flower and add a yellow stamen dot. Dry-brush leaf highlights with yellow-green overstrokes.

Wild Phlox

1. Place stems and calyxes with yellow-green plus a touch of white. Filbert brush petals are pink tipped with white. Use a variety of pink hues for added interest.

2. Detail the flower center with a short curved stroke of dark red. Add many short leaf strokes to each stem.

3. Place a tiny yellow dot at each center. Add dark green leaf strokes to stems, and dry-brush calyxes with dark red.

Tansy

1. Stroke stems and leaves with a liner brush using light and medium value greens. Place flower heads with a small filbert brush double-loaded with Cadmium Yellow and Antique Gold.

2. Shade stems and leaves with dark value green. Dry-brush shading on flower heads with Olive Green.

3. Highlight flower heads with dabs of light value yellow. Dot Olive Green in the centers.

◐ Wild Strawberry

1. Stroke stems and leaves with liner brush. Dab flower centers with Olive Green.

2. Place flower petals with a filbert brush loaded with pale green tipped with white. Base the berry with yellow blended into orange.

3. Strengthen the flower petals with overstrokes of white. Shade the berry with a floated edge of orange using a flat brush.

◑ Wood Violet

1. Place stems with a yellow-green. Establish heart-shaped leaves with a double-loaded filbert brush. Stroke the back flower petals with dark value violet hues.

2. Place side petals with a middle value tipped with dark purple to produce a streaky stroke.

3. Stroke the front petal with a light value tipped with a medium value. Vein the leaves with light green.

◑ Nasturtium

1. Establish petals with wavy crescent strokes using a flat brush double-loaded with yellow and orange. Keep the orange edge of the brush facing the flower center. Fill in round leaf shapes with yellow green.

2. Continue to add wavy crescent stroke petals. Line the leaves with dark green veins.

3. Float-shade leaf edges with a dark value green.

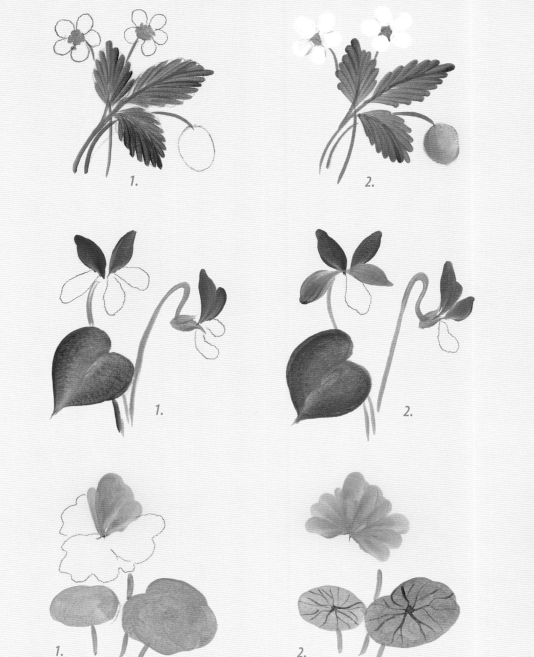

4.

5.

6.

4.

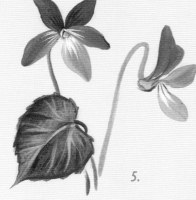

5.

6.

4.

5.

6.

○ Wild Strawberry

4. Pull Olive Green detail lines outward from the flower centers. Float-shade one side of each leaf with dark value green. Float red along the outside edges of the berry.

5. Tap flower centers with dabs of yellow; add tiny green leaves between the petals and at the berry stem. Add tiny brown seeds to the berry.

6. Detail the flower centers with brown pollen dots. Dry-brush white highlights on the leaves and berry.

● Wood Violet

4. Detail back petals with dark purple vein lines. Add white detail lines to the side and front petals. Outline and detail leaves with dark value green.

5. Place a yellow stamen dot at flower center. Float-shade along the center vein of the leaf with dark value green.

6. Violets can be found in colors ranging from white to deep purple. There's even a yellow variety.

● Nasturtium

4. Shade and separate the petals with floated color using a mix of Burnt Sienna plus orange. Detail the petals with Burnt Sienna spots.

5. Highlight petals and leaves with dry-brushed white. Add a yellow stamen dot to front-facing flowers. Loosely outline wavy petal edges as needed.

6. Nasturtium petals are edible and add color to salads and garnishes. Paint them in bright yellow and red hues!

● Mint

1. Stroke in framework for stems and leaves with a gray-green hue. New growth at the top of the stem is smaller and lighter in color. Begin the leaves at the tip with a single stroke pulled outward from the center vein, then pull remaining strokes inward to form the leaf shape.

2. Using an angular bristle foliage brush, stipple the flowering areas with purple and red-violet. Add dry-brushed accents to the leaves and stems with these same colors.

3. Stipple highlights onto flowers with light value purple and accent with touches of white. Dry-brush white highlights on the leaves for a silvery shimmer.

● Chicory

1. Place stems and calyxes with gray-green. Stroke underlying petals with medium value blue-violet using a small flat brush.

2. Layer additional petals with light value blue-violet plus white.

3. Detail the petals with fine lines of blue-violet. Stipple the flower center with medium and light value blues and add tiny dark blue liner brush strokes to define the edges. Shade the stems and foliage with gray-green plus a touch of blue-violet.

1.

2.

3.

1.

2.

3.

Wild Marjoram

1. Stroke the framework for the stems with Raw Sienna. Place small leaf strokes at the base of each stem branch. Stipple mounded flower tufts with medium value pink.

2. Shade the flower tufts with dark pink. Stipple the tops with a light value. Begin to dry-brush subtle green shading on the stems.

3. Detail the tops of the flower tufts with tiny white and pale pink florets using the tip of a small round brush.

Chives

1. Place stems and leaves with long, double-loaded liner brush strokes using contrasting green values. Apply and release pressure on the brush to create the look of twisted and turned leaves. Dry-brush round "spiked" flower heads with medium value purple and red-violet hues.

2. Pull liner brush strokes outward from the flower center to define a cluster of individual petals.

3. Build up layers of petal strokes gradually becoming lighter in value at the center of the cluster. Highlight with strokes of white.

Queen Anne's Lace

1. Place stems and framework with light and middle value greens using a liner brush. Stipple the flower head shape with middle value green using an angular bristle foliage brush.

2. Stipple the flower head area with white, leaving open spaces for a lacy effect. Develop the leaves with comma strokes pulled inward to the stem.

3. Detail the floret clusters with tiny dots and dabs of thick white paint. Let dry. For added interest, accent the flower with touches of transparent pink, yellow or violet.

Goldenrod

1. Stroke stems and framework with light and middle value greens. Using the angular bristle foliage brush, stipple the flower texture with green along the top of each branch beginning at the base and moving toward the tip.

2. Stipple flower texture with Cadmium Yellow and Antique Gold double-loaded onto the foliage brush. Place thin-thick-thin leaves with middle and dark value greens using a round or liner brush.

3. Highlight flower texture with Yellow Light plus a touch of white. Add veins, detail lines and shading to the leaves and stems with dark green.

1.

2.

3.

1.

2.

3.

● Pink Yarrow

1. Place stems and framework with light and middle value greens using a liner brush. Base small round florets with a thin color wash leaving a "hole" in the center of each. Dab a touch of Antique Gold in the centers.

2. Add several small individual petals to each floret using a small round brush with middle and dark value pink hues. Fern-like leaves are stippled with light and dark value greens double-loaded onto a flat brush.

3. Highlight the top-facing petals with lighter value pinks. Add tiny white dots to the centers. Let dry. Tint the centers randomly with accents of Yellow Light. Yarrow may also be painted in shades of yellow, pale green or red for interesting filler in floral arrangements.

● Lavender

1. Stroke stems and framework with light and middle value greens. The foliage may be completed in this one step. Dab clusters of filbert brush "buds" at the top of the stems with middle value purple.

2. Add a layer of dark purple buds.

3. Highlight the clusters with the filbert brush double-loaded with light value purple (lavender) and white.

● Purple Coneflowers

1. Establish the stems to determine the direction of the flower. Base the flower center with thinned Burnt Sienna using short overlapping brushstrokes. Place each petal with two long liner brush strokes using a medium value red-violet hue.

2. Detail the petals with long fine lines of dark value red-violet. Fill in the spaces at the base of the petals with short strokes of green.

3. Highlight the petals with dry-brushed overstrokes of white plus a touch of pink.

4. Float-shade around the base of the petals and over the base of the completed cone with dark value red-violet.

5. Strengthen the highlights on front-facing petals with additional dry-brushed white.

6. To paint the coneflower center:

   • Base the cone with Burnt Sienna using short overlapping strokes.

   • Shade with strokes of Burnt Umber toward the center and at the bottom.

   • Highlight with dabs of Antique Gold.

   • Float thinned red-violet along the bottom and shaded edge. Add final highlight dots.

1.

2.

3.

4.

5.

6.

1.

2.

3.

4.

5.

Black-Eyed Susan

1. Establish stems to determine the direction and placement of the flowers. Base the centers with Burnt Umber. Place the petals with thin-thick-thin strokes using a round or liner brush loaded with Cadmium Yellow and tipped with Antique Gold.

2. Stroke petal vein lines with a mix of orange plus Antique Gold. Fill in the spaces at the base of the petals with short green strokes. Darken center by dabbing with additional Burnt Umber.

3. Float-shade and separate the petals with a thinned orange plus Burnt Sienna mix using a side-loaded flat brush. Shade the center with a mix of Burnt Umber plus Payne's Gray.

4. Highlight the petals with dry-brushed overstrokes of white. Highlight the centers with touches of Antique Gold.

5. Accent the highlights with transparent Yellow Light plus a touch of Cadmium Yellow.

● Bachelor's Buttons

1. Place long stems and leaves using a liner brush double-loaded with light and middle value greens that have been toned with a touch of white and blue. Stipple the flower center with purple.

2. Define each petal with three or four liner brush strokes pulled outward from the center using blue-violet plus a touch of white.

3. Overstroke the petals with a lighter value blue-violet. Tap this color onto the center also.

4. Continue to develop the center with short upright strokes of a lighter value blue. Define the front-facing petals with a "star" shape.

5. Detail the petals with dark blue-violet vein lines pulled outward from the center. Front-facing petals have veins pulled from the center of the "star." Add purple detail strokes around the outside edges of the flower center.

6. Float-shade blue-violet at the base of each petal where it connects to the flower center. Highlight random petal edges with dry-brushed accents of white.

1.

2.

3.

4.

5.

6.

Field Poppy

1. Stroke long stems using a liner brush double-loaded with light and middle value greens. Place "fan stroke" petals using a round brush fully loaded with Cadmium Yellow and tipped with orange.

2. Detail petal veins and pull strokes outward from the center with a mix of Burnt Sienna plus orange. Loosely outline the petals to define ruffled edges. The leaves are formed with a series of thin-thick-thin strokes.

3. Float-shade with orange to separate the petals and create flipped edges. Shade the stems and detail the leaves with dark green.

4. Deepen the strokes at the base of each petal with overstrokes of Burnt Sienna. Place a short Olive Green stamen highlighted with yellow at the center. Add four small detail strokes of Burnt Sienna protruding from the top of the stamen.

5. Dry-brush white highlights on the petals, stems and leaves using a filbert brush.

6. Accent the highlights by brushing with transparent Yellow Light.

◗ *Field Daisy*

1. Place stems to determine the direction and angle of the flowers. Using a round brush, stroke in every other petal in the underlying layer with pale green tipped with white.

2. Stroke the remaining top-facing petals in the same manner adding more white for contrast.

3. Shade, separate and pull detail lines at the base of the petals with thinned Antique Gold using the knife edge of a side-loaded flat brush.

4. Highlight the petals with heavy white overstrokes using a round or liner brush, allowing much of the under-painted colors to remain visible.

5. Brighten front-facing petals with additional white strokes.

6. To paint the daisy center:

   • Base with Antique Gold.

   • Establish form with Cadmium Yellow and orange.

   • Shade with Burnt Umber.

   • Highlight with white. Note the angle of the center in relation to the direction of the stem.

1.

2.

3.

4.

5.

6.

Pasture Rose

1. Place each petal with two "fanned strokes" using either a round or a large filbert brush. Load the brush generously with light pink and tip the brush with dark pink to create streaks. Base the center with Antique Gold.

2. Separate the petals by floating dark pink along the underside of overlapping edges. Double load a filbert with Cadmium Yellow and dark pink and stipple the oval-shaped center.

3. Shade the base of each petal with dark pink using the knife edge of a side-loaded flat brush. Deepen the center shading with Burnt Umber.

4. Highlight overlapping petal edges with white plus a touch of pink using a side-loaded filbert brush. Highlight the centers with Cadmium Yellow and white pollen dots.

5. To paint the rose hips and sepals:

   • Base with yellow-orange gradating into red.

   • Detail with Burnt Umber.

   • Shade top edge with a red wash; shade lower edge with dark red.

6. Pull sepals from the bud end of the rose hip with toned green. Add dry white highlight. Dry-brush final white highlights on the pink rose petals. Float tints of dark pink here and there on outside edges. Spaces between petals are stroked with green. Leaves and stems may be placed with yellow-green during the first stage of painting. Float dark value green shading and dry-brush highlights. Stems and smaller leaves are strokes of yellow-green and dark pink.

These flowers speak of springtime, renewal and joy. Paint them with either a bright or pastel palette in the colors of your choice. Spring bulb catalogs are great resources for photographs of flower varieties and colors. Combine bulb-type flowers with budding branches and add other elements such as little bees, birds, eggs and nests to paint a complete picture story of the return of spring.

Bulb Flowers

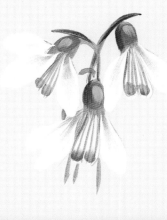

● Crocus

1. Lightly outline the individual petals with thinned color. Place back or interior petals with light color values using filbert brush strokes.

2. Stroke the side petals with light and medium values double-loaded onto the brush. Keep the lighter color along the outside edge of each petal.

3. Complete the front-facing petal with a light color value. Add vein details with dark color using a liner brush and thinned paint. Note the gradual transition of color from the flower into the stem.

4. Separate and shade the individual petals with floated color using a flat brush side-loaded with thinned dark color value.

○ Snowdrops

1. Establish stems, calyxes, and the base of each outside petal with a middle value green on a liner brush. Stroke the two lower petals with white.

2. Add heavy white overstrokes to each petal using a small round brush or a no. 4 liner. Detail the two lower petals with vertical green stripes.

3. Highlight calyxes and stems with light green. Shade and separate the stems with a bright green hue. Detail the tips of the striped petals with additional touches of green.

4. Float shading at the base of each petal as needed for contrast or to separate flowers in a group. Use a very small amount of thinned color such as a mix of green plus Payne's gray plus a touch of white.

1.

2.

3.

Wood Hyacinth

1. Sketch the main stem with yellow green using the liner brush. Place bell-shaped flowers in your choice of medium value hues using round brush strokes. Note that the white flowers are placed with a soft green color.

2. Overstroke the flowers with petals of a lighter value by adding white to the original color. Leave some of the first layer showing at the opening of each bell.

3. Detail the bell openings with dark color values, using a short liner brush to define the tips of the petals where needed. Shade the stems with darker green hues. Dry-brush highlights on the front-facing petals with white.

Quick Tip

To keep the light, open feeling of these delicate flower clusters, limit the amount of foliage you place with them. Leaves and stems are placed with long, grassy strokes using a liner brush. If needed, review the section on painting leaves with a round brush on pages 22-23.

● Tulip

1. Begin by placing the inner and back petals with medium and dark values using a double-loaded filbert brush. Place the shading along the under side of overlapping petals.

2. Add the outer and front-facing petals with the double-loaded brush, placing the lighter color along the top side of overlapping edges. Blend the area with light, form-following strokes, maintaining adequate contrast between light and dark color values.

3. Add vein details to the petals with a liner brush as shown. Use a dark color value for contrast against the petal color. Begin at the stem and pull strokes upward, branching out toward the tip of the petal.

4. Deepen the shading along the inside edges near the flower base with floated color.

5. Dry-brush soft white highlights here and there on ruffled edges and front-facing petals.

1.

2.

5.

3.

4.

1.

2.

3.

4.

5.

◗ Daffodil

1. Place underlying petals with medium yellow. Base top petals and trumpet rim with a light layer of white.

2. Stroke the top petals with light and medium color values double-loaded onto a filbert brush. Keep the light color value to the outside edges of each petal.

3. Brush the base and inside the throat of the trumpet with orange (medium value color).

4. Complete the trumpet edges with a lighter yellow-orange hue. Add vein details as shown with a liner brush using a darker color for contrast.

5. Separate the petals and shade the throat of the trumpet with floated color. Use yellow-orange against the yellow petals. Use red-orange to deepen the throat of the trumpet. Stamen details are added with heavy touches of yellow.

✳ Quick Tip

You need not strive for solid coverage when painting flower petals. Allow light to pass through the semi-transparent layers, reserving the heaviest paint for final details and accents.

● Iris

1. Side and back-facing petals are stroked with darker color values using filbert brush strokes. Note that the side petals are composed of "unfin-ished" strokes allowing light to pass through the center of each petal.

2. Place front-facing petals with lighter color values.

3. Begin to develop details on the lower petals by adding secondary petals and by placing white on the "beard."

4. Add petal veins and outlines. Float-shade the inside edges with a dark color value to separate petal layers and add contrast.

5. Dry-brush highlights with white. Accent the "beards" on the lower petals with yellow and touches of orange.

1.

2.

3.

4.

5.

Cyclamen

1. Place the back petals with medium and dark color values double-loaded onto a filbert brush. Keep the darker value along the underside of overlapping petals.

2. Stroke front-facing petals with medium and light values keeping the lighter color along the outside edges.

3. Add vein and detail lines to the petals. Place the ruffled center opening with small "C" strokes using a side-loaded flat brush.

4. Shade and separate the petals where needed with thin washes of floated color.

5. Float highlights on front-facing petal edges with a light color value. Dry-brush with accents of white where more contrast is needed.

Quick Tip

Cyclamen stems are a unique burgundy red color. The flowers may range from white and pale pink to deep, cool red-violet hues. Their variegated heart-shaped leaves have a soft velvet texture which is created with layers of dry-brushing.

● Anemone

1. Depending on your choice of background color, red flowers may first need to be underpainted with white. Establish the center with a dark blue-black color by tapping with the point of a round brush. Petals are placed with "unfinished" filbert brush strokes pulled from the outer edge of the petal inward. Use the knife edge of the brush to pull the unfinished strokes inward toward the center.

2. Place petals with red and pink double loaded onto a filbert brush, keeping the lighter color on the top-facing edges. Blend colors lightly to form each petal.

3. Shade and separate individual petals with floated color using a dark red hue.

4. Dry-brush highlights onto top-facing petals with white. Pull short, heavy white strokes outward from the center.

5. Complete the center with heavy textured pollen dots using black and yellow as shown. Add brilliance to the red flower by brushing the petals with a thin wash of pure red.

1.

2.

3.

4.

5.

1.

2.

3.

4.

5.

Dahlia

1. Place petals with a filbert brush loaded with light color and tipped on one edge with a touch of medium color to establish overlapping petals.

2. Stipple the center area with yellow and orange hues.

3. Shade and separate individual petals with floated color. Use the knife edge of the brush to pull shading detail strokes outward from the center.

4. Dry-brush highlights with white overstrokes.

5. Add remaining details, color tints and final highlights. Place short petal strokes around the flower center using a double-loaded filbert brush. Detail and separate these petals with a fine liner brush. Float transparent color washes here and there to illuminate the petals. Define petal edges with heavy white liner brush strokes.

● *Orange Tiger Lily*

1. Place each underlying petal with two strokes of a filbert brush following the contours of the outside edges. Double-load the brush with yellow-orange and orange, keeping the darker value toward the outside edges of the petals.

2. Place the alternating top-facing petals in the same manner, but this time keep the lighter value toward the outside edges of the petals.

3. Fill in the turned petal edges with yellow-orange. Stroke contour-following vein lines with a mix of orange plus burnt sienna using a liner brush. Add detail spots with burnt sienna loaded onto the tip of the liner brush. Note how the spots appear much smaller near the tip of the petal. Place a long green/burnt sienna pistil into the flower center.

4. Float-shade and separate the petals with burnt sienna using the corner of a flat brush. Two or more thin layers may be needed for best results.

1.

2.

3.

4.

Orange Tiger Lily

5. Highlight with dry-brushed over-strokes of white using a filbert brush.

6. Tint the highlights with thinned light yellow. Float-shade petal edges here and there with accents of red/orange. Stroke long stamens and filaments with a liner brush and add "bean-shaped" anthers at the tips of the filaments with short, heavily textured strokes.

White Lily

7. A white version of the lily can be painted using the same step-by-step instructions as for the Orange Tiger Lily. For steps 1 through 4, use combinations of warm white, Olive Green, and Olive plus a touch of Payne's Gray to establish the light, medium and dark color values. Use Titanium White for layered highlights.

Pink Stargazer Lily

8. This stargazer lily follows the same basic steps using white and a "cool" red (such as DecoArt's Santa Red) to mix the pink values. Red plus a touch of Payne's Gray makes a splendid shading/detail hue. Wiggle the brush as you place the petal strokes to make ruffled edges.

Flowering vines are ideal for border motifs. *They can also be added as graceful filler in combination with other flower types. Once you've mastered the liner brush techniques for graceful vines and tendrils, why not "freehand" a running vine motif along a wall border? Or try framing a window or doorway with a softly rendered flowering vine in your favorite colors.*

Vining Flowers

Honeysuckle

1. Establish the curving vine with golden brown tones using a liner brush. Leaves are placed in sets of two at the base of each flower cluster. Petals are stroked with a beige/flesh color using a round brush.

2. Overstroke top-lying petals with white.

Bittersweet

1. Establish the vine and berry stems with golden brown and green mixed in the liner brush.

2. Place ripe berries with orange and red-orange applied with your finger tip or with a standard round pencil eraser dipped into the two colors. Unripe berries are antique gold and golden brown.

Virginia Creeper

1. Establish the vine with golden brown and burgundy red mixed together in a liner brush. Base each leaf section with multiple round brush strokes of yellow-green pulled outward from the center vein.

2. Stroke in the vein lines and loosely outline each leaf with dark green.

Honeysuckle

3. Highlight selected flowers with additional overstrokes of white. Overstroke "fading" flowers with pale yellow. Add long stamens with white and golden brown.

4. Float tints of orange onto the tips of yellow petals. Place small leaf strokes at the base of each flower cluster.

Bittersweet

3. Develop shading and details on vines and leaves. Highlight unripe berries with dabs of yellow.

4. Add hulls to ripe berries with short, heavy strokes of antique gold and yellow. Tint vines and leaves here and there with orange.

Virginia Creeper

3. Float dark green along the center veins and at the base of each leaf section.

4. Float a variety of red and burgundy tints on the tips of the leaves.

Quick Tip

Bittersweet and Virginia Creeper make great "filler" for autumn borders and flower arrangements.

● *Climbing Rose*

1. Stroke the thorny vines with golden brown plus a touch of red. Tender bud stems are placed with yellow-greens. Establish the initial placement and shape of the rose with medium and light pink hues. Apply the colors with a filbert brush using a loose, swirling motion keeping the edges soft and dry.

2. Create the look of layered petals by overstroking the rose form with white using thin-thick-thin liner brush strokes. Note how the strokes are small and short at the center and long and wavy around the outside edges.

3. Tap yellow and golden brown pollen into the centers of open roses using the point of a small round brush.

4. Float-shade the center and lower edges of the rose with tints of dark red.

5. Highlight several front-facing petals with white overstrokes. New growth stems and leaves are stroked with light and medium value yellow-green hues double-loaded onto a filbert brush. Leaf details can be placed with a dark green value. For interest, add some filler leaves with yellow-green and rose pink double-loaded on a filbert brush.

1.

2.

3.

4.

5.

1.

2.

3.

4.

5.

Blackberry Vine

1. Stroke the thorny vines with a mix of golden brown plus a touch of red. Place the berries and the flower centers with a light coat of yellow-green.

2. Outline the individual segments of the mature berries with a red-violet hue. Outline unripe berries with green. Stroke the flower petals with a variety of light pink hues using a filbert brush.

3. Float-shade around the edges of ripe berries with red-violet. Float-shade the unripe berry along its lower edge with green. Shade the base of each flower petal with dark pink.

4. Detail the flower centers with short strokes of yellow and antique gold. Along the undersides of the ripe berries, float tints of purple or dark red-violet to deepen the shading.

5. Highlight each berry segment with a dot of white. The highlighted segments near the center of each berry should receive an even brighter highlight. Highlight the flower petals with white overstrokes. Detail the centers with tiny dark pollen dots.

● *Clematis*

1. Place petals with medium and light color values double-loaded onto a filbert brush. Use two wavy strokes for each petal, keeping the lighter color toward the center of each.

2. Detail the petals with a medium value using liner brush strokes. Tap the center with the knife edge of a small flat brush which has been double-loaded with yellow and red.

3. Shade and separate the petals with a dark value using floated color.

4. Dry-brush white highlights onto the petals using a filbert brush. Stipple the center with touches of white. Large, mature leaves are formed with wavy strokes similar to those used for the petals. Small new leaves are placed with single double-loaded strokes. Add tints of the flower color to completed leaves for unity and added interest.

1.

2.

3.

4.

1.

2.

3.

4.

Morning Glory

1. Fill in the basic flower shape with medium value blue using a filbert brush and pulling "fan" strokes from the outer edge downward toward the base of the trumpet.

2. Place three long thin-thick-thin liner brush strokes in white as shown. Pull shorter white strokes upward from the trumpet base.

3. Establish the front edge of the flower. Sketch it in with chalk pencil or trace and transfer the shape of the front section to the Step 2 painting. Beginning at the center and moving outward to the left and right, fill in the section with short curved strokes. Continue with "unfinished" strokes part way around the perimeter of the flower. Pull two white overstrokes over the front lip to complete the open edge of the trumpet.

4. Float around the outside edges with pure, transparent blue. Accent the trumpet center with a floated tint of yellow.

Quick Tip

Try painting these trumpet-shaped blossoms in a variety of blue, violet and pink hues. Tilt the flowers at different angles and connect them with vines and tendrils. We could also use these same basic steps to create petunias!

● Trumpet Vine

1. Establish the vine and stems with yellow-green and raw sienna. Place the sepals (bud jackets) with strokes of raw sienna and red-orange. Base the trumpet and back petals with red-orange plus a touch of white.

2. Place front-facing petals with yellow-orange.

3. Float-shade the throat and the base of the trumpet, and separate the petals with a mix of burnt sienna plus a touch of red. Shade and separate sepals with floated edges of green.

4. Dry-brush white highlights on all petals and down the center of the trumpet. Detail the centers with yellow stamens.

5. Brush transparent tints of yellow and yellow-orange over all highlighted areas.

1.

2.

3.

4.

5.

Jasmine

1. Establish the vines and stems with golden brown and green mixed in a liner brush. Place buds and tubes with medium and light values of rosy pink. Note the long thin shape of the tubes. Stroke petals with a filbert brush using a variety of pinks. For a variegated stroke, load the brush with one color and "tip" the bristles with a different value. Pull the strokes inward toward the center.

2. Float a small "C" stroke of antique gold into the throat of each flower. Note the placement of the stroke in relationship to the direction the flower is facing. Shade and deepen the throat with dark rose.

3. Highlight random top-facing petals with dry-brushed strokes of white.

Quick Tip

A pleasing warm, coral pink hue can be made by mixing red-orange plus white. Although in nature, jasmine vines have dark green foliage, be sure the leaves in your painting are kept light and airy so as not to overpower the delicate blossoms.

I've selected both common and exotic species of filler flowers for the illustrations in this section. These elements are intended to play a supporting role in your flower paintings, adding fullness, visual weight, balance and direction to your compositions. Gardening encyclopedias and seed catalogs make great references. Filler flowers should be placed purposefully so as not to detract from the main flowers in your design.

Filler
Flowers

Astilbe

1. Establish the stems and framework with fine liner brush strokes.

2. Double-load the brush with light and medium color values side-by-side. Here we see a pink flower and a white flower. The white flower is placed with white and yellow-green.

3. Highlight with additional layers of lighter color and white until you have enough contrast and brightness in relationship to the surrounding flowers in your composition.

Quick Tip

These feathery flowers grow on tall, straight stems and are really easy to paint using an old "scruffy" flat brush or an angular bristle foliage brush. Remember to keep astilbes light and lacy with lots of open spaces for light to filter through.

1.

2.

3.

1.

2.

3.

1.

2.

● Sea Holly

1. Mix blue-green plus white to create the base color for leaves and stems. Use a no. 4 short liner for all steps. Place the stem with the base color and red-violet double-loaded onto the brush. Pull blue-green leaf and petal strokes outward from the stem. Establish the short petals around the flower head with dark purple plus a touch of the blue-green mix.

2. Fill in the flower head with dark purple. Add veins and details to leaves and stems with purple.

3. Overstroke the flower head with short strokes of blue-green and white. Highlight front-facing leaves with dry-brushed white strokes. Tint the base of the flower head with red-violet.

● Sea Lavender

1. Establish a framework of fine branches with the blue-green mix.

2. Place tiny lavender buds onto the branches using the knife edge of a no. 2 filbert brush double-loaded with purple and white.

3. Highlight buds with additional dabs of white.

● New England Asters

1. Place the stems and basic leaf shapes with middle value greens. Dab flower centers with yellow and green. Pull short, straight petals inward toward the center with violet on a small round brush.

2. Pull more petals with red-violet hues using a small round or a liner brush. The bud is just five strokes pulled toward the base.

3. Highlight petals with overstrokes of a lighter value. Brighten the centers with yellow and orange, and add white pollen dot details.

● Garden Phlox

1. Establish stems and basic leaf shapes with middle value greens. Place flower petals with pink hues using short filbert brush strokes.

2. Detail the centers with dark red, pulling short strokes outward from the center. Float dark red at the base of each bud.

3. Float dark red along the edges of some of the petals. Float white highlights on the edges of the front-facing petals. Detail the centers with pale yellow stamens.

1.

2.

3.

1.

2.

3.

1.

2.

3.

4.

5.

◗ Alstromeria

1. Establish stems and basic leaf strokes with light yellow-green hues. Brush the center of the large back petal with yellow. Base the remaining petals with a mix of white plus red-orange (a pale coral hue).

2. Detail the petals with red-orange vein lines. Add dark red spots to the back petal using the knife edge of a no. 2 filbert brush.

3. Float tints of red-orange around the outside edges of all petals.

4. Float dark red in the flower center, at the bottom of the back petal.

5. Dry-brush white highlights on front-facing petals. Add long yellow and yellow-green stamens with liner brush strokes.

✳ Quick Tip

Filler flowers and leaves should not overpower the main elements of your composition. Keep the colors soft and slightly transparent, allowing light to filter through the layers of color.

● Cattails

1. Place the stems and grassy leaves with neutral light brown tones using a liner brush. Stroke the cattail form with a filbert brush then pat into the wet paint with the flat side of the brush to create a textured effect.

2. Float-shade the edges of the cattail with a burnt umber, again patting into the wet paint for more texture.

3. Stipple a textured highlight toward the center of the form. Pull some random detail strokes at the top and on the sides. Shade the stem with burnt umber.

● Wheat and Grain

1. These are developed with golden yellows and natural browns. Stems and grassy leaves are placed with long, thin-thick-thin strokes using a long liner brush.

2. Paint the grain heads with short strokes of a double-loaded round brush. A no. 4 mid-liner is also a good brush to use.

3. Detail lines and shading of individual grains are overstroked with dark brown. Additional "beard" lines may be added with antique gold and raw sienna.

1.

2.

3.

1.

2.

3.

Ferns

1. Place stems and framework with a no. 4 short liner brush. Leaves are placed with the same brush loaded with olive green and tipped with dark green. Apply the strokes with a wavy "thin-thick-thin" motion.

2. Highlight the stem and vein the leaves with a light yellow-green hue. Add floated tints of orange or red to the tips of several leaves.

Ivy

1. Establish vines and stems with browns and greens using a liner brush. Place leaf shapes with a flat brush double-loaded with light and medium value greens.

2. Add veins with dark green. Float dark green along the center veins and randomly on the leaf edges.

Little things mean a lot! *Tendrils, dew drops, ribbons, butterflies and bees...even a little bird...add interest and give life to your floral creations. In this section you'll also find ideas for using transparent color glazes to add harmony, balance and illumination to your finished painting. You'll be amazed at what a few finishing touches can do!*

Finishing Touches

Curlicues and Tendrils

1. Load the liner brush with a generous amount of thinned paint. Hold the brush nearly perpendicular to the surface allowing the paint to flow freely from the point of the brush.

2. Graceful thin-thick-thin lines combined with fine tendrils and comma strokes make interesting filler for more formal compositions.

3. These liner brush strokes begin with fine, curved lines and end with sudden pressure to form a droplet at the end of the stroke. They are very graceful and airy.

4. Bare branches add interesting texture and line to any seasonal bouquet. Keep each line segment straight, adding pressure to the brush to form a little bud before changing the direction of the branch.

Ribbons and Bows

These ribbons and bows are formed with a series of thin-thick-thin "S" and "C" strokes. Each twist of the ribbon is placed as an individual stroke. The blue ribbon is created with a flat brush double loaded with a darker and a lighter value of blue. The pink ribbon is also a darker and lighter value applied with a no. 4 short liner. Highlight the center of each stroke where the ribbon reflects light with dry-brushed white for added dimension and softness.

1. *2.* *3.* *4.*

1.

2.

3.

1.

2.

3.

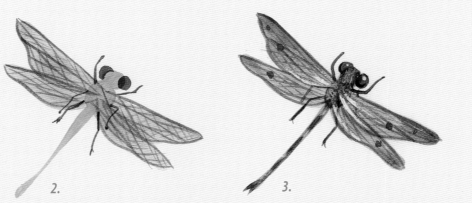

1.

2.

3.

◖ Bees

1. Place the head and upper body section with black or another dark value. Base the lower body with solid antique gold and stroke the wings with a wash of antique gold.

2. Tap fuzzy stripes on lower body and stroke legs with black or a dark value.

3. Float-shade the lower body section with raw sienna. Overstroke the wings and add an eye with white. Detail as needed for contrast against the background.

● Butterflies

1. Place wings with slightly thinned paint for transparency. The underside of the wing is usually duller in color. Note the size and shape of the body.

2. Add details to the wings and body with a fine liner brush.

3. Float shading where the wings attach to the body. Dry-brush lightly with white to highlight the wings' edges.

● Dragonfly

1. Place the head and body with yellow-green. Stroke wings with transparent color wash using a filbert brush.

2. Detail the wings and add legs to the underside of the body with fine lines. Big eyes are characteristic of this creature! There are also no antennae.

3. Shade and detail the body by dry-brushing with a darker green value. Highlight the wings with dry-brushed white. Add bright detail spots to the wings and eyes.

● Water Droplets

1. Outline the droplets with white. Think about the natural shape and placement of the water drop as it rests or cascades down the object.

2. Float a dark value of the background surface color along the top edge and below the bottom edge of the droplet.

3. Float a thin white highlight on the droplet along the bottom edge. There should be sharp contrast between highlight and shadow along the bottom edge of the droplet. Add tiny white sparkle dots near the center of the drop reflecting the light source in your composition.

● Weathered Leaves

1. Place leaves with slightly thinned paint leaving holes and ragged edges. Old, faded leaves should contain golden hues.

2. Add veins and detail lines.

3. Shade along the center vein and outside edges with floated color. Outline and detail the holes and tears with dark brown.

● Turned Leaves

1. Indicate the exposed underside of the leaf with a lighter color value.

2. Complete the top side of the leaf with details and shading.

3. Place veins on turned leaf with a light color. Shade with only slight tints of color. Develop sharp light/dark contrast along the folded edges.

1.

2.

3.

4.

● Songbird

1. Establish the main outlines and place the eye and beak with thinned burnt umber using a liner brush.

2. Place the main body areas with washes of color using a filbert brush, allowing the outlines to show through.

3. Overstroke the wing and tail feathers with raw sienna and burnt umber double-loaded onto a no. 4 short liner brush.

4. Build up white areas with heavy pure white. Overstroke fine feathers on the breast with lighter color values. Add fine details to the face and head, and place the eye with burnt umber. Stroke final details on wing feathers and add a highlight to the eye with white.

✳ Quick Tip

Elements such as this sweet little bird add life and energy to floral compositions.

● *White Rose with Color Glazing*

Who can resist the queen of the garden, a fragrant white rose? For this beauty I chose a grayed violet tone for the underpainting and shading in order to reflect the lavender background color. Other alternatives might include muted yellow-greens, golden yellow or rosy beige. The amount of depth your flower has depends on the degree of contrast between light and dark color values.

Fill out the simple rose motif with leaves, ferns, and delicate filler elements in a variety of colors and textures.

1. The rose is composed of a series of double-loaded flat brush strokes. This "blown apart" illustration shows how the individual strokes are formed.

2. Establish the flower's basic form as a sphere with a shaded depression at the center. Keep the edges soft and loose.

3. Place layers of short double-loaded petal strokes at the back and into the center of the rose. Place larger petals around the outside edges, varying the pressure on the brush to create ruffled strokes. Keep the light color value toward the outside edges.

4. Finish the middle of the flower with layers of overlapping petals. Additional petal strokes may be added for fullness. When the layers are dry, highlight the front-facing petal edges with several heavy floats of white.

1.

2.

3.

4.

● Final Glazing Technique

Soft transparent glazes and final white highlights give this rose an inner glow!

The term "glazing" refers to the application of transparent washes of color over the completed painting. Glazing is done before any finishing such as varnish is applied.

For controlled tinting, such as along leaf and petal edges and to illuminate highlights, begin with a dry surface. For best results use colors whose pigments are transparent (such as yellow light). Side-load a flat or filbert brush with thinned paint and float the transparent color where desired.

For an overall effect on broad areas, brush the dry painting with a thin, even coat of a liquid acrylic extender such as DecoArt Easy Float in water. The surface should appear only slightly shiny with no puddles or drips. Side-load a large flat brush with thinned color and brush the color here and there onto the wet surface. The extender will pull the color, allowing it to fade out softly around the edges. The color can be further softened by dusting lightly with a large, soft mop brush.

● *Orchid with Color Glazing*

The exotic orchid with its graceful lines is an elegant motif for the cover of a personal journal or wedding album. Position a delicate dragonfly to balance the design.

Orchids can be found in many varieties and colors. Refer to horticultural magazines for inspiration and follow this simple step-by-step technique as a painting guide.

1. Place back petals with medium and light values blending the light color toward the base of the petals.

2. Place top-lying petals in the same manner, working around the stamen area if possible.

3. Add veins to the petals with dark color value. Shade and separate the petals with floated dark value. Basecoat the stamen area with white.

4. To complete the stamen, basecoat with medium yellow and shade with yellow-orange at the center. Add a pattern of dark red spots as shown. Highlight with touches of white. The exposed roots at the base of the plant are based with a dull antique gold hue and detailed with burnt umber. Moss filler is loosely scumbled in with muted browns and then detailed with curly lines.

1.

2.

3.

4.

● Final Glazing Technique

In the previous White Rose demo, we learned how a final glazing of transparent color enriches and deepens the white tones for a more natural look. The same glazing technique can be applied to any color of flower, even colors as bright as shown on this orchid. In the final glazing step, leaf highlights are illuminated with transparent yellow-green and tints of red are added to reflect the flowers. Touches of violet in the shadows give added depth.

The glazing palette used for the orchid is:

Reds

Light Value: White + a touch of Napa Red

Medium Value: Napa Red + White (1:1)

Dark Value: Napa Red

Yellows

Light Value: Yellow Light

Medium Value: Cadmium Yellow

Dark Value: Cadmium Yellow + a touch of Napa Red

Greens and Blues

Warm Middle Value: Yellow Light + Black Forest + White (4 : 1 : a touch)

Cool Dark Value: Black Forest Green

Shadow Accents: Blue Violet + Napa Red

Browns

Light Value: Antique Gold

Dark Value: Burnt Umber

99

Let's gather some favorite blossoms into bouquets, wreaths, garlands and borders. These arrangements can be painted by following the easy step-by-step illustrations for the individual flowers shown throughout the book. You can use the patterns provided or create your own designs by using the patterns as a guide. Enlarge or reduce the designs to best suit your requirements.

"Merrily, merrily, shall I live now, under the blossom that hangs on the bough."

—William Shakespeare,
1564 – 1616

Floral
Compositions

Flower Borders

Trace the line drawing on page 118 and transfer to your painting surface. See page 11 for information on using tracing paper, transfer paper, and a stylus. Keep the lines faint and brief, eliminating most of the details. Using the transfer lines as a guide, lightly sketch in the design with thinned paint and a liner brush. Let dry. Erase any telltale transfer lines using an art eraser.

With a liner brush, lay in a framework of stem lines on which to place the flowers and leaves. Develop the individual flowers using the step-by-step illustrations shown earlier in this book. The borders shown here are, from top to bottom:

A. Chrysanthemums

B. Wildflowers and Herbs

C. Violets and Ribbon

D. Sunflowers

A.

B.

C.

D.

Completed Flower Borders

A. Chrysanthemums in warm autumn hues can be combined with colorful leaves, grasses and other elements for a seasonal border.

B. Wildflowers and herbs make wonderfully quick and easy borders. Here I've chosen pink coneflowers, chicory and coreopsis.

C. Violets and a ribbon are always a pretty combination. For added interest, paint violets in many values from dark to light, using colors that range from purple to red violet to blue violet. Little white dots used as filler among the flowers add a delicate touch.

D. Sunflowers can be used in so many ways! This design can be repeated end to end and used as a border, turned at a right angle to form a corner, or used as a central motif.

A.

B.

C.

D.

Wildflower Wreath

1. Trace the line drawing on page 119 and transfer to your painting surface. See page 11 for information on using tracing paper, transfer paper, and a stylus. Keep the lines faint and brief, eliminating most details. Loosely outline the main design elements of the wreath with thinned light brown paint and a liner brush. Stipple background foliage behind the flowers with soft green and blue-green hues, adding some of the background basecoat color into the mix as a toner.

2. Referring to the corresponding step-by-step illustrations shown earlier in this book, establish the initial petal placement of each flower. The colors and flowers used here are:

   Yellow: Field Poppies

   Pink: Pasture Rose

   White: Queen Anne's Lace

   Blue/Violet: Asters

   Purple: Violas

   Red: Yarrow

3. Develop the individual flower details, petal veins and centers. Place shadows with floated color.

Completed Wreath

Add leaves and vines to fill out the wreath. Dry-brush highlights where needed to soften the petals. Accent the flowers and leaves with transparent glazes to illuminate and unify the design. Final details such as pollen dots and tendrils complete the painting.

Quick Tip

Now that you've seen how easy it is to paint a beautiful wreath like this, try creating your own wreath design. Start by sketching onto tracing paper two concentric circles which represent the outer and inner perimeters of your wreath. Divide the double circle into three equal sections. Develop your flower layout within one section only, then repeat your design two more times to complete the circle. Choose flowers in a variety of sizes, colors and textures for maximum interest, leaving ample space between flowers for leaves and filler elements.

● *Autumn Gathering*

This autumn bouquet gathers together late summer garden flowers, wildflowers, vines and grasses.

The complementary color scheme of yellow and violet with filler elements in warm oranges and browns captures the mood of the harvest season. Even the busy little bee helps to depict the "gathering time" theme.

The colors and flowers used are:

Yellow: Black-eyed Susan

Violet: New England Asters

Orange: Bittersweet Vine

Browns: Cattails, Grains and Grasses

1. Trace and transfer the line drawing on page 120 to your painting surface. Lightly outline the main elements with a golden brown hue using thinned paint and a liner brush. Stipple the spaces between the flowers with the golden brown using an angular bristle foliage brush. Allow some of this background filler to spray gracefully outward from the center of the composition.

2. Develop the individual elements of the design following the step-by-step illustrations shown earlier in this book. Your colors may be adjusted depending on your choice of background color.

3. Complete the final details and add dry-brushed highlights. Apply the brightest highlights to any top-lying petal edges, especially on the largest yellow flower, to help bring it forward.

● **Completed Autumn Gathering**

Bring the painting to life with final glazes of color and added details. Illuminate the brightest top-lying petals with yellow light. Back-facing petals can be tinted with cadmium yellow.

Dry-brush touches of purple/blue-violet mix at the base of shaded petals. Stroke long dried grasses with natural golden brown tones using a liner brush to fill in any empty areas.

Spring Garlands

Garlands are the perfect size and shape for painting on a variety of surfaces, especially furniture, small areas of wallspace such as over doorways and windows, cabinet doors, and more.

Trace the line drawing on page 121 and transfer to your painting surface. Keep your lines faint and brief, eliminating any details. Using the transfer lines as a guide, lightly sketch in the design with thinned paint using a liner brush.

Develop the individual flowers and leaves using the step-by-step illustrations found in this book as a guide. For a fresh look, keep your work light and airy in the initial stages. You may choose to change the flower colors to match the background of the surface you're painting.

The three garland designs shown here are:

A. Spring bulbs.

B. Mixed garden flowers.

C. Roses and lavender.

Note that the larger flower types are placed in the centers of the garlands, while the ends taper off with smaller-petaled flowers.

A.

B.

C.

◗ Completed Spring Garlands

A. These spring bulbs include daffodils, tulips, crocus and snowdrops, and are combined with fine bare twigs to form an early spring motif.

B. The late spring/early summer garden flowers in this garland are chosen for their variety of size, shape and color. Here I've used a white daisy, a purple pansy, yellow buttercups, pink phlox, and two varieties of blue forget-me-nots.

C. Roses and lavender combine into a romantic Victorian theme for this garland. I've chosen vining roses for this design, but a more formal variety could be used just as effectively. Use several different leaf types and colors to add variety and interest.

A.

B.

C.

◗ *Color Wheel Bouquet*

The flowers in this bright bouquet are arranged in the form of a classic color wheel and use a basic triangular shape as a design format. The colors and flowers used are (clockwise from the top) :

Yellow: Sunflower, Coreopsis, Goldenrod

Orange: Daylily

Red: Cosmos, Coreopsis, Zinnia, Anemone

Violet: Zinnia, Aster

Blue: Hydrangea, Anemone, Delphinium

White/Green: Cosmos, Wedding Phlox, Coreopsis, mixed foliage.

1. Trace and transfer the line drawing on page 122 to your painting surface. Lightly outline the main elements with thinned light brown paint and a liner brush. Fill in the spaces between the flowers with a variety of cool greens using a filbert brush. Use short, diagonal strokes, allowing some of the background filler to spray gracefully outward from the center of the composition.

2. Develop the individual flowers in the design following the step-by-step illustrations shown earlier in this book. Your colors may be adjusted depending on your choice of background color. If you're working on a darker background, the flowers may need to be underpainted with white before applying color. Begin to complete the final details and add dry-brushed highlights. Apply the brightest highlights to any top-lying petal edges.

◗ Completed Color Wheel Bouquet

Bring the painting to life with final glazes of color and final details. Add a variety of grasses, leaves and tendrils to fill out the design. Deepen the shading and add stem details in the spaces between the flowers. Illuminate the final painting with glazes of transparent color. Enhance yellow and orange flowers and centers and add a glow to white areas with yellow light. Add tints of warm and cool reds to leaf edges. Enhance shadows and strengthen blue flower petals with blue-violet. Glaze leaf highlights with yellow light plus a touch of green (a transparent yellow-green mix).

● Mixed Floral

Any number of flower types can be combined for an exciting display of color. Choose a variety of shapes, sizes, colors and textures to create interest. The little bird breathes life and adds freshness to the design.

The colors and flowers used are:

Yellow: Dahlias and flower centers

Reds and Pinks: Rose, Garden Phlox, Alstromeria

Blues and Violets: Iris, Morning Glory, Asters

White: Daisies

1. Trace the line drawing on page 123 and transfer to your painting surface. Keep your lines faint and brief. Using the transfer lines as a guide, lightly outline the main elements with thinned golden brown paint and a liner brush. Dry-brush the spaces between the flowers with a mix of golden brown plus a touch of Ever-green on a filbert brush. Allow some of this background filler to spray gracefully outward from the center of the composition.

2. Develop each flower following the step-by-step illustrations shown ear-lier in this book. Your colors may be adjusted depending on your choice of background color. When working on a light background, try adding a touch of the background color to all the colors on your palette.

3. Complete the final details and add dry-brushed highlights. Apply the brightest highlights to any top-lying petal edges.

Completed Mixed Floral

Stroke a variety of grasses, leaves, vines and branches to fill out the design. Deepen the shading and add stem details in the spaces between the flowers. Bring the painting to life with final glazes of color. Illuminate the yellow flowers and centers and add a glow to white areas with yellow light. Add tints of warm and cool reds to leaf edges and daisy petals. Cool shadows with blue-violet. Glaze leaf highlights with yellow light plus a touch of green (transparent yellow-green mix).

Give the gift of flowers!
Paint your favorite flowers on watercolor paper to use as cutouts for greeting cards, bookmarks, jewelry, altered art projects or papercraft embellishments. Simply paint, seal with acrylic varnish and trim with a craft knife or decorative edge scissors. If you enjoy working with a computer, scan your painted design into any popular picture editing or scrapbooking program, then print out copies of your art to use for stickers and tags. It's amazing how even little "practice" flowers can be transformed into works of art!

Greeting cards

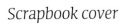

CONSIDER
THE LILIES OF
THE FIELD, HOW
THEY GROW;
THEY TOIL
NOT, NEITHER
DO THEY SPIN.

MATTHEW 6:28

Candle wrap

Gift tags

Painted mat

Collage

Bookmarks

Keep Life Simple

Papa Newcomb
Boothbay Harbor, ME
1945

Line Drawings

Flower Borders, p. 102-103

These line drawings may be hand-traced or photocopied for personal use only. They are shown here at full size.

Wildflower Wreath,
p. 104-105

This line drawing may be hand-traced or photocopied for personal use only. It is shown here at full size.

Autumn Gathering, p. 106-107

This line drawing may be hand-traced or photocopied for personal use only. It is shown here at full size.

Spring Garlands, p. 108-109

These line drawings may be hand-traced or photocopied for personal use only. They are shown here at full size.

Color Wheel Bouquet,
p. 110-111

This line drawing may be hand-traced or photocopied for personal use only. It is shown here at full size.

Mixed Floral, p. 112-113

This line drawing may be hand-traced or photocopied for personal use only. It is shown here at full size.

Text Index

31.

31.

31.

33.

33.

33.

34.

Visual Index

This handy visual index is designed to help you quickly and easily find the flowers you want to paint, even if you don't know their names! The numbers in the lower left corners are the pages where you'll find the step-by-step instructions.

43.

46.

46.

46.

50.

51.

51.

52.

58.

59.

62.

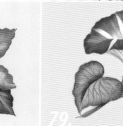

62.

63.

64.

65.

75.

76.

77.

78.

79.

80.

81.

88.

89.

89.

92.

92.

93.

93.

The best in art instruction and inspiration is from North Light Books!

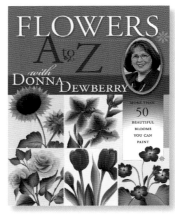

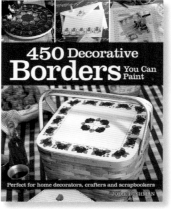

Flowers A to Z with Donna Dewberry
Painting your favorite flowers is easy and fun with Donna Dewberry's popular one-stroke technique! You'll see how to paint more than 50 garden flowers and wildflowers in an array of stunning colors. Discover Donna's secrets for painting leaves, vines, foliage, flower petals, blossoms, and floral bouquets. Add beauty and elegance to any project including furniture, walls, pottery, birdbaths and more!
ISBN-13: 978-1-58180-484-3; ISBN-10: 1-58180-484-9, paperback, 144 pages, #32803

Painter's Quick Reference: Flowers & Blooms
When you're in a hurry for painting help, here's the book to turn to for ideas, instruction and inspiration. With more than 50 step-by-step demonstrations, *Painter's Quick Reference: Flowers & Blooms* shows you how to paint your favorite flowers, including apple blossoms, lilies, lilacs, poppies, roses, orchids, irises, pansies and many more. Use this special guide to jumpstart your creativity, improve your strokework, or explore new mediums—including acrylics, watercolors, oils and gouache.
ISBN-13: 978-1-58180-761-5; ISBN 1-58180-761-9, paperback, 128 pages, #33430

450 Decorative Borders You Can Paint
Simple strokes. Fabulous borders! It's easy and fun to add the perfect touch to every painting project with the charm and beauty decorative borders. Just follow Jodie Bushman's step-by-step instructions and let your creativity do the rest. With *450 Decorative Borders You Can Paint*, you'll find 12 start-to-finish projects, 32 beautiful borders you can paint in just 3 easy steps, and hundreds of borders, corner treatments, medallions and other designs you can copy outright or adapt to your own painting projects.
ISBN-13: 978-1-58180-691-5; ISBN-10: 1-58180-691-4; paperback, 128 pages, #33326

Painting Nature
Discover the delightful details of nature in this stunning new book by internationally acclaimed artist and teacher, Peggy Harris. From a perfectly posed butterfly to a delicately tinted leaf to tiny eggs in a bird's nest, natural details enhance any painting's appeal. With tips, more than 50 step-by-step painting demonstrations, fascinating facts and her own beautiful artwork, Peggy teaches you to observe nature accurately and let your knowledge give life and credibility to your painting, no matter what your artistic style.
ISBN-13: 978-1-58180-715-8; ISBN-10: 1-58180-715-5; paperback, 128 pages, #33382

These books and other fine North Light titles are available at your local arts & crafts retailer, bookstore, or from online suppliers.